The Price of Admission

The Price of Admission

Embracing a Life of Grief and Joy

————◇————

Liz Petrone

Broadleaf Books

Minneapolis

THE PRICE OF ADMISSION
Embracing a Life of Grief and Joy

Cover image: Alice G. Patterson
Cover design: James Kegley

Print ISBN: 978-1-5064-5878-6
eBook ISBN: 978-1-5064-5879-3

to my mother, of course

Contents

Prologue

The Decorative Apple

Let me tell you a story.

I'm sixteen years old, sitting in the kitchen with my mother while she makes dinner. And just for purposes of context here, let me also tell you a little about me at sixteen: I'm a hot mess. I'm drinking. I'm drugging. I just got my heart truly broken for the first time by my first love. I cannot bear to be in the same room as my mother most of the time (and honestly I think the feeling is mutual). And I'm starting to feel things—big and heavy adult things, like pressure and inadequacy and pain and depression and anxiety—and I'm convinced I'm so amazingly special that I'm the only person on the whole planet who has ever felt these things. Basically, I'm out of my mind and terrified.

And then, on top of everything else, I've stopped eating, which at this point isn't even a conscious decision as much as it is a misguided coping mechanism. I certainly don't realize then that I'm probably starving myself in an attempt to slow down or even reverse time, to carve the new curves out of my body and keep me a kid a little while longer, where life felt simpler and less lonely. No, at this point all I know is that obsessing over food and my body feels a heck of a lot easier than actually facing anything else I'm feeling.

Anyway, so there I sat in the warm kitchen, watching my mother make dinner. I'm sure I was supposed to be doing my homework or something else, but I don't remember any of that. I just remember watching her. And God, was she a sight. If I was a hot mess (and I was), she was my polar opposite; fresh from her big job in a power suit with full makeup, big shoulder pads and bigger diamonds. She'd been commanding rooms since well before I was born and the kitchen was no different; it was hers and I was a visitor, desperately trying to shrink myself into the corner. By then things were tense between us most of the time, and in the kitchen it was so quiet that the click of her heels on the hardwoods rung out like a heartbeat.

"Are you okay?" she asked me, finally, probably weirded out by my staring. And isn't that the question, right there? Was I okay? I was not okay, and I was sure she could see that if she just stopped and looked, like really looked at me, my dilated pupils and the hollows under my eyes from not sleeping, the way all of the weight I'd lost made my clothes hang off of me, the protective way I'd hunch my shoulders around my heart and try to curl up into the smallest configuration of myself as possible.

But I lied, told her I was fine. Of course I did because that's what we do, right? I'd already learned at sixteen that in order to survive–in order to remain upright and breathing and presentable–I needed to hide some things, paint over some things, suck some things in and swallow some things down.

Some things were to be avoided, like food or truth, and others were to be flat out denied. So I let my chance go by and I lied, and instead of looking at her in the face, I let my focus rest on the kitchen table in front of me, and more specifically, on the ever-present bowl of apples in the center of it.

This bowl of apples was a fixture in our house, and they were not for eating. They were the best apples, the biggest, shiniest, roundest Granny Smith green apples specially picked to sit in this blue bowl on the kitchen table, catching the evening light through the window and looking perfect. (If you wanted to eat an apple, the ordinary ones—the ones just for eating—were in the fridge.)

Gosh it sounds ridiculous now to say that, but it was just the way it was. I was sixteen and a hot mess and kind of a jerk, and I decided right then that I was going to eat one of those decorative apples right there in front of my mother just because I could, because the air in the kitchen had filled with the smell of olive oil and garlic, and all I could think about was how I was just so very hungry. This isn't surprising—in every memory of high school I have I am hungry as hell, except "hungry" probably isn't even the right word. It's more of a deep emptiness, a lack of something that goes well beyond food and even biology and edges itself into this idea of not enough, never enough. It's an emptiness that I will carry with me in some fashion for most of my life, an emptiness that despite all the work and all the wisdom that has come I still wrestle with, even now as an adult the same age my mother was in that kitchen all those years ago.

So I found the best apple, the shiniest and the roundest and the greenest of them all. I picked it up and turned it around and around in my shaking hand to find the best first bite, and just as I brought it up to my mouth, it cracked clean in half in my hand. The two pieces fell open onto the table; the inside of that perfect apple was rotten, all brown, soft, mealy, and gross. I spent a long time looking at it lying on the table in front of me, smelling that sickly sweet fermentation smell, remembering how perfect it had looked on the outside, convinced there was a message there for me. And there was a message in there, all right, something big. I wasn't old enough yet or ready enough then to get it, but I felt the edges of it tugging at me anyway. I looked from that rotten apple to my gorgeous mother; the heartbeat of her heels still clicking around the kitchen.

It had looked so perfect.

———◊———

We lost my mother five years ago to suicide. It was, as these things often are, totally unexpected. In the first few days after it happened, people just kept coming up to me: her friends, her neighbors, her coworkers, even her family, saying the same things over and over again:

"But she was so perfect."

"She was so beautiful."

"She was so together."

And what did I remember? The apple. I thought of that decorative apple and how it had been picked for display and never for function, and I realized that maybe the thing that had tugged at me as I sat there in the kitchen, smelling garlic and holding a rotten apple, was this idea of how what we show the world on our outside doesn't always match what's actually going on in our inside.

Right? Our outsides can lie. They can lie the same exact way that we do, the way we've learned to lie when people ask us if we are okay and we say, "No, really, I'm fine, it's fine, everything is *fine*," when maybe the truth is we are dying a little inside. The way I was already lying all those years ago at sixteen, starving and drinking and hiding the truth away. The way my mother maybe lied her whole life, hiding everything going on deep inside and out of sight. The way we've created a whole culture out of making ourselves presentable, perfect, shiny, and filtered, and sometimes no one really knows what's going on inside until it's too late.

When my mother died and it was time to plan the funeral, the priest asked if he could talk openly about suicide during the funeral mass.

Yes, of course, I said, remembering the apple.

No, of course not, everyone else said, aghast. What will people think?

So what the priest talked about instead was this same idea of suffering. Quiet suffering. Private suffering. Carefully hidden suffering, wrapped up in the dark corners of our lives. It was the suffering my mother had carried her whole life and no one really knew, the same suffering I starved myself to get away from, both of us convinced we were the only ones who felt the way we did. It was, the priest said, the kind of suffering that kills people.

He didn't know us personally, not well anyways, so he couldn't have known about that time we had come home to find my mother drunk, unresponsive, lying in her underwear on the bathroom floor. How we'd called 911 and an ambulance came, and we'd waited next to her in the emergency room for what felt like forever, willing her to please open her eyes, wondering the whole time if this was it, if this was how she was going to die. How when she did finally open her eyes, the first thing she wondered before even asking what had happened was if the neighbors had seen.

But I guess he didn't need to know that because he heard that story or others like it a thousand times before, I'm sure. Because what I've come to see is that in some variation it's a universal story, one that has been ingrained into so many of us, one that we can see reflected back to us plainly every day in our politics and our celebrities and our communities and now in our Instagram and Facebook feeds. It's the story of a society that's painted itself over in the hard shellac of perfection and tamped the real truth of our lives down deep inside of ourselves where it can sit, hidden, and fester.

I think back to that day in the kitchen, and sometimes I wonder still what would have happened if my mother and I had opened up to each other right there. Could we have saved each other? It's a slippery path, that regret, and I can feel it threaten to pull me under. I could have told her the truth when she asked me if I was okay. I could have asked her to tell me hers. I could have said, "We can do this. We can carry each other. You are not alone." I didn't. But I can say it to you.

There's not much I know for sure. I have four amazing children, and my parenting style is basically me making it up as I go along and praying a lot. I've been married for fifteen years; occasionally, someone will ask me for marriage advice, and I'll just stare at them like a deer in the headlights, because I'm not kidding you when I say every day I wake up and see my husband next to me and think "wow I literally cannot believe he is still here." I still don't know how to apply eyeliner, I've burned everything I've ever tried to bake, and my house is the place plants come to die. And while I get closer every single day, I still don't know what I want to be when I grow up.

I tell you this because I want you to know there is no way I would sit down here and write something that tells you how to live your lives or how to raise your babies or how to find the meaning of life. There is really only one thing I know for sure, one thing I believe in wholeheartedly and enough to write a book about, and that is what I wish I had said to my mother: We can do this. We can carry each other. You are not alone.

I know all too well what it's like to muddle around in that darkness alone, and I know what it's like to lose somebody in that place forever. I know this too: that feeling of quiet desperation, the voice that tells you that no one could possibly understand, is lying to you. I hear from women every day who tell me how they feel less than or broken or like they are doing something—or everything—wrong. Women who carry that same not-enough hunger I wrestle with. Women who have learned that same lesson I learned at sixteen, which is that in order to survive we need to hide our truths. The messy and the ugly and the painful don't fit nicely into our conversations at school pickup or in the grocery aisles so they need to be avoided, stuffed down and hidden not just from each other but worse, from ourselves.

Which is, of course, probably the worst and most dangerous thing we can do. There's tremendous power in speaking up and speaking out and speaking truth. If quiet and hidden suffering is the kind of suffering that kills people, speaking up is, I have no doubt, what can save us.

The first time I told the truth was shortly after my mother died. I don't remember what I said but I know it was inelegant and weird and terrifying and then freeing and after I caught my breath, amazing. In fact, it was so amazing that I got a little over-excited and decided from that moment on I would tell my truth to anyone who would listen: clerks in coffee shops or the person pumping my gas, the waitress taking my drink order, the guy who goes through our recycling bins each week looking for returnable cans. And if that wasn't weird enough, I also started asking people to tell me theirs. I'd corner my friends or the parents of my kids' friends or people I saw in the grocery store who I thought I recognized from the neighborhood and ask them how they were doing and then basically not accept "I'm fine" as an answer.

And yeah, it was super weird. People looked at me like I was crazy and let me tell you: if it's human nature to want to keep our stories to ourselves, it's even more human nature to not want to tell them to a crazy person. But I knew the stories needed to be told. I remembered the priest's homily. I remembered the decorative apple. And I knew this was how we saved lives, even if it was too late to save my mother's. Maybe I could save someone else. Maybe, even, I could still save myself.

So I sat down and I started writing. I had no training and no idea what I was doing except one guiding rule: I wanted to tell the truth, no matter what. I made a blog and I started telling stories to my fifteen followers, and it felt like the only true work I had ever done towards healing the hole in my life. And then people started to respond, and a community grew out of that. There is one thing now that I know for sure: telling the truth has changed everything.

The stories in this book, like this one, are pieces of a life. They're the lessons I've learned in between the moments of great pain and indescribable beauty. I tell them to you for two reasons: one, so you know you are not alone in any of this; and two, because simply, they are the truth. And telling the truth will set us free.

1

———◊———

Everything Is Not Going
to Be Okay

It was 2002, I was twenty-one years old, and I'd had too much to drink. Again. It happened sometimes, and this time it happened the way it always did: out with my then-boyfriend Nick, something we intended to be a quick in and out, and then all of the sudden five hours had gone by and I was doing something stupid like standing half-naked in a parking lot trying to convince him that even though it was Tuesday, we should just stay out all night, dance, and let loose. Let go of what, I'm not entirely sure. I had no children yet, no house to pay for or clean, no wrinkles, and my mother was still alive, yet for some reason I still desperately needed an escape. From myself, probably. It kills me now to think of how we wasted all that incredible child-free time we had stretched out in front of us by drinking cheap draft beer and listening to bad music instead of sleeping—like I would just die to do now—but back then it was just what we did. It was all we knew. And by we, I mostly mean me, because Nick's priorities were already starting to shift towards being a contributing member of society. I just lagged a little further behind, as usual.

"I have to work tomorrow morning," he said, unmoved by my attempts at persuasion. "Actually, come to think of it, so do you." He has a way of punctuating sentences with his eyebrows that, depending on my mood, is either adorable or incredibly irritating. When they came together as he looked down the bridge of his nose at me, I did not find it cute, not one bit, not at all.

I shrugged. "I can go in late. They won't even notice." It was a lie, and a bad one at that. Of course they would notice. I cringed at the way I sounded—like when I was a little kid begging my health-nut mom for one of the desserts in the restaurant's pretty glass case—but I also wasn't quite ready to give up. The night was young and so was I and I was drunk, sure, but I could still mostly talk without slurring if I concentrated hard. Plus I thought I looked pretty decent despite the booze. My pre-four-babies-body was still halfway dressed up from work. My respectable cardigan shed somewhere around the third beer when I had loaded the jukebox and started dancing, and in my hand were my heels that had come off not long after. Now we were standing outside of the bar that he was trying to convince me to leave, and it was colder than I remembered it being outside. I shivered so hard I lost my balance, stumbling as the gravel of the parking lot bit into my bare foot. I yelped.

"At this rate, you're not going to be able to go anywhere."

I sighed. He was right. I always had hated this part of the night. Booze had such a lovely way of making me light and flirty and chatty and all of the things I wasn't naturally, and too often I had so much fun once I started that I didn't want to stop. I was freshly out of my teens, had just started my first real job, and was on the wrong side of a little too old for this, but I wasn't quite ready to let the college party lifestyle go, either. Either way, of the two of us, I was always the last one to want to settle in and go home for the evening.

When I think about it now, it's this idea that there was always something more, something better waiting around the corner in that next bar, that next beer, that next bad decision. It's a gaze–partly because I was young but maybe even more so because I was human–that is permanently squinting forward towards the horizon instead of looking around myself at what was right in front of me. I was standing there buzzed up and shivering in a gravel parking lot with the man I was going to someday marry and my shoes in my hand, sure, but I wasn't really *there*.

I tried to pull it together. "No, you're right," I said, draping my arms around his neck and leaning into him, half suggestively and half because I wasn't exactly steady on my feet. "Let's go home and go to bed."

———◊———

When Nick and I were first dating, we would sit and talk about the "not okay" for hours on end, dissecting everything that was wrong with us and our parents and the establishment in general, wasting time and making plans to change the world just as soon as we were old enough or the beer ran out, whichever happened sooner. I'd always tried to walk the fine line between making sure he knew I was a little broken inside without ever actually appearing broken enough to scare him. Back then I kept most of my real shit stuffed down deep into the darkness inside of me, and I was afraid if I let him see all of it—if I actually did, say, *let go*—he'd run away as fast as he could. So instead, I let the truth out in little hiccups when it got too big to keep in, a pressure release to keep me from exploding.

He'd asked me once during one of those marathon sessions what my wildest fantasy was. I'd looked at him, smiled, and asked: "You really want to know?" He nodded, eager, and so I leaned in close, lowered my voice, and told him how I wanted, more than anything, for someone to tell me that everything was going to be okay convincingly enough that I believed it. I knew from the way his face fell that this answer was not exactly the kind of thing he was anticipating, but it was, to my credit, the truth, and it was what I'd stood out in that parking lot asking him to chase with me in the next drink or the next bar or the next adventure: this idea that eventually, hopefully soon, everything was going to be okay.

Everything is going to be okay. Just saying it out loud gives me goosebumps. But what a pile of magical bullshit, am I right? We've all bought into this idea that everything can and should be okay, and then the truth looks more like this: It's probably going to be okay, eventually, for a while. And then it's going to be not okay for a while, maybe a long while, and just when you can't stand it a moment longer and you're about to buckle, it will slowly start to get okay again. And then one day you will wake up and realize it is okay. Kind of. Until it isn't again, and the whole cycle repeats itself.

And, well, those words of comfort don't exactly roll off the tongue, do they? So even if it's a lie I've said it countless times to everyone I love, and even more to myself, *everythingisgoing tobeokayeverythingisgingtobeokayeverythingisgoingtobeokay*, an optimistic mantra to get through awkward phases and job losses and bad breakups and bad hair days and hangovers like the one I knew I'd have the next morning if I didn't go home right that second.

When we got home, I changed out of my work clothes and into something warm and went into the only bathroom of the apartment Nick and I shared, a craptastic mess of a space so small that I had to sit on the toilet to be able to see myself in the mirrored medicine cabinet. The lighting was awful, overhead and fluorescent and harsh, and when I sat down and saw my reflection I cringed. I looked awful. I was drunk and disheveled and my makeup had started to smudge into raccoon rings around my red eyes. I washed my face and brushed the beer out of my teeth before I noticed that my foot was still bleeding from where I'd cut it in the parking lot. I'd left a bloody footprint on the floor tile.

"Jesus, Liz," I thought to myself, hearing it in my mother's voice. "You're a mess." Trying not to let myself entertain the idea of how much bacteria was on my bathroom floor and therefore now also in my foot, I rummaged in the medicine cabinet for a bandage and some antibiotic ointment and a couple ibuprofen to hopefully cut what was sure to be a throbbing ache in both my foot and my head in the morning. There was a plastic baggie on the part of the second shelf where Nick kept his stuff—a toothbrush and a stick of deodorant and some dental floss, he wasn't complicated—filled with the familiar white pills. I took two, stepped down onto my foot and winced, and took a third for good measure. Everything is going to be okay.

"What were you doing in there?" Nick asked me when I climbed onto the bed. "I was starting to worry you had passed out."

"Cleaning up my foot. Oh, and I took some of your ibuprofen," I said. "I want to have a fighting chance of making it to work on time tomorrow."

"My ibuprofen?" He looked confused. His eyebrows went up in the form of a question.

"Yeah, in the plastic baggie in the medicine cabinet."

He was quiet for a second, then threw back the covers and walked quickly to the bathroom. From where I was laying I could hear the sounds of him rummaging around in the cabinet.

He came back with the baggie in his hand. "These?" he asked, waving it at me.

"Geez, Nick," I said, "you don't have to wave it in my face. I'm drunk, not blind. Yes. Those."

"Liz. These are prescription painkillers."

"Wait. What?"

"Yeah."

"Not ibuprofen?"

"Nope. Not even close."

"Shit," I said, my heart speeding up a little. "I took three."

My heart started to beat even faster as this sunk in. "Is that bad, do you think? It can't be good. Not after all that beer. Oh shit. Nick. Shit." My palms started to sweat. I was panicking. I was surprised by the way the unmistakable feeling of having been here before hit me, hard.

"I'm sure it's fine," Nick said. I could tell he was trying to keep me calm, which should probably have been endearing but just wound me up even further. We might be wasting my last precious minutes on earth sitting in this god-awful apartment. I was not dying here. We needed to act fast.

"How do you know that? Do you even know what you are talking about? Because I do! I've been down this road, Nick. I almost died once before. I know what this is. Maybe you should call 911? I bet I will need my stomach pumped! You better call my mother. I'll pack my stuff." I jumped down from the bed too hard and my foot protested. I buckled, sank to the floor and leaned against the wall, my head in my hands, trying to breathe.

Weird gaspy sounds were coming from me. My chest hurt, and there was a ringing in my ears. I wondered if this was what a heart attack felt like, and I wondered too why Nick was still just standing there. "Do something," I wheezed at him.

He stood up from the bed. "Hold on." He left again, and I heard the low murmur of him on the phone but couldn't make out what he was saying.

"Is that my mom?" I yelled out to him. "Tell her to meet us at the ER." The last time she'd been there at my side the whole time, which was funny because we could hardly stand each other back then.

Nick came back and lifted me onto the bed. "It's all good," he said. "That was poison control. I told them everything, and they said the particular combination you took shouldn't be toxic." He pulled the covers up around me. "Try to relax."

I inched close to him and rested my head on his shoulder. My heart was still thumping away like a jack hammer in my chest. I wondered if he could feel it. "Then why can't I breathe?"

"Panic attack?"

"Great. That's attractive."

I waited for him to say it, wondered if he even remembered, willed him to lean in and whisper those six little words everyone wants to hear when they're mid-panic attack: everything is going to be okay. But he didn't say that. "I'm here," he said instead.

I'm not sure how long we laid there waiting for my breath to come back, but eventually it did, and with it the full weight of the realization that maybe he didn't say everything is going to be okay because it probably wasn't, not in the way the sentiment implies anyway. He and I were planning to marry each other and to start a whole adulthood together, and we both knew in our hearts that there was no actual way everything was going to be okay, not all of the time, not forever. We didn't know then how not okay it would sometimes get, and I wonder if we had if we would have ever been able to make ourselves step into it. But what he did say, "I'm here"? It's actually kind of genius. It always works. It's the truth that is left over when we've lived through the rest long enough to know that maybe it's not ever gonna be the kind of okay again that it used to be before.

It's what I try to say now when "everythingisgonnabeokay" rings as hollow as it is, to the people I love when they are struggling or lost or depressed or grieving or any other flavor of just not okay. It's what I say to myself pretty much all of the time, when I drag my tired ass out of bed in the morning and what I say when I drop it back in there much too late at night, a micro prayer, half awe and half thank you, a love letter penned to the universe and to God and yes, to myself when I was eighteen, after I tried to take my own life.

Which was, then, probably the only story that I hadn't yet told Nick. I felt the ring on my finger. If we were really going to do this, I couldn't keep all of my darkness hidden inside forever. I picked my head up and looked at him. The light next to the bed was switched off but the room was lit from the one working streetlight outside and the occasional flashing lights of a police car speeding by. "I want to tell you a story," I said.

"Okay." He shifted, turning to face me.

"When I was eighteen I tried to kill myself," I said. And I told him again about the things he already knew, how I had stopped eating when I was sixteen and fell deeper into the clutches of anorexia than I had ever intended to, losing too much weight and most of my friends and my mother and ending up too sick and too frail to go away to college after graduation, even though I had tried. And then I told him the parts I hadn't told him yet, about how when I drove myself home from school in a U-Haul, my mother had told me to keep right on going because I wasn't welcome in her house anymore. So I had taken myself to a series of places looking for a place to rest, including my father's and a rehab hospital and eventually, the bottom of two pill bottles.

He didn't say anything the whole time I talked, but he didn't stop touching me either. His hand was as firm on my back as his gaze was on my face, and he hadn't closed his eyes or recoiled or pulled back like I had always assumed he would when I told him.

"I only have one question, and you don't have to answer it if you don't want to."

I nodded.

"Did you really want to die?"

I took a big breath. That was the question, wasn't it? Had I wanted to die? I had asked myself the same thing almost every day in the days and weeks and months after, as I slowly climbed out of the hole of anorexia and depression that I had been in. The thing is, I wasn't really sure anymore of the answer. I had tried again and again to remember what it had felt like to be in that moment, what that desperation felt like physically. Had I felt it in my body? Was it like this panic attack I had just had, where I shook, sweated, lost my breath, felt my heart pound in my ears? I couldn't remember. "I don't know." I was going to leave it at that, and that would have been enough for him, but it wasn't enough for me. Maybe it was the drinks I had had or maybe it was the painkillers or maybe it was just the exhilaration of having set down the secret I had carried, but I wanted him to understand, even if I didn't. "I don't know if that matters, really. I don't know as if it's actually even about wanting to die. What it was about, I think, was not caring anymore about living. Does that make sense?"

I think about this a lot, actually, even more so after my mother ended up taking her own life. And the thing I return to again and again is that idea that while everything is maybe never always going to be okay, things are very likely going to get better. And inevitably time has this way of erasing pain from your memory until it just seems like a dull throb in the background and not the agonizing darkness it had once been. I can physically remember the sensation of standing there with the second bottle of pills in my hand, empty because I had taken them all as fast as I could before I lost my nerve and changed my mind. I can remember how one pill must have fallen out of my hand when I pushed them all into my mouth and sat there in the wetness at the bottom of the sink, dissolving slow into something softer and smaller, just as I wanted to. I know what I was wearing, and the way the covers felt as I pulled them up around my shoulders and waited for whatever was coming. But I cannot, no matter how hard I try, remember what the pain felt like. I can't recall the way the heartbreak had split my chest open and my insides felt like they had poured out of me until I was hollow, an empty shell. I can't remember the ambivalence about something as precious as this one crazy and beautiful life. And it's the not remembering, when you think about it, that is the real gift. Pain comes, yes, but if you can hang on long enough, eventually you won't be able to remember what it felt like when it was there.

I thought I was special back then too, that my pain was extraordinary, unnatural even, which maybe is what you inevitably believe when everything being okay is always the ultimate goal. I thought I was alone, that no one could ever have understood the way I felt. I recognize these now for what they are: the lies that the darkness tells you. But then, I bought them hook, line, and sinker, always trying to run from the pain with every ounce of strength I had, with food or with deprivation, with exercise, with booze. With distraction and isolation and boyfriends and TV and eventually, with my life.

A little time and distance though, and the light makes plain the truth: pain comes with joy. It's the labor before the birth, the night before the dawn, the storm that soaks the soil before the bloom. You can't let one in without the other either, this I now know. I tried for years, wrapping myself up in a big protective sheet of bubble wrap and bouncing around the edges of my life, playing at being human until it almost killed me, or until

I almost killed me. Because that's the lesson, really, the only takeaway worth anything that came from that mistake. You can't run away from pain and live. The not-okay is as much a natural and necessary part of life as the okay. They are not opposites, not even close: the pain is just the other side of the same life coin.

And this life shifts fast, doesn't it? As I write this, we have four beautiful babies that were each just a gleam in my eye when I laid in the arms of the man I would marry and told him my truth and he told me in response the only real truth he could: I'm here. And now at bedtime sometimes, I brush the hair from our babies' foreheads and whisper it, say "I'm here" into their sleeping ears like I'm saying thank you, because I am. I'm thankful for the things I haven't missed, and for the grace and forgiveness of that failure. For the way the ceiling of my joy has adjusted itself every year since then and made space for every new incredible thing I have been able to take in, including the pain. Yes, even that. Because while everything is certainly not okay, not even close, that doesn't mean this life isn't beautiful.

So how could I ever have risked this, I will sometimes ask myself. What arrogance could have convinced me that I knew better than God did, that whatever I was feeling at the time was big and deep enough to let it swallow me whole and throw away the gifts yet to come? But then that's not the whole truth either, at least not anymore. That's the truth as seen through the eyes of a married mother of four in her late thirties. It's the truth seen from a woman who sought help, eventually, who did the work, eventually, and who found some semblance of peace in her family and her friends and her yoga practice and her marriage and her words, eventually. It's the truth of a woman who has put enough distance between herself and that suicide attempt to look at it as what it was: what happens when the late-night-only-in-the-dark kind of worry crosses over into the daytime where it doesn't belong and blots out all of the light.

I'm come to realize that the true lie the darkness tells is one of omission. The darkness doesn't tell you how pain is simply the price of admission. And it's a steal, really, a bargain. One I will pay a hundred times over for the simple pleasure of a beautiful sunrise or a mug of tea heavy in my hands or another mile run or a hug from a longtime friend or the smile of my child across a crowded room. For the comfort of my soon-to-be-husband's arm strong across my waist while he watched me sleep. For the moments when the darkness whispers its lies in the night and I am able, still, to answer it with the only two words that matter: I'm here.

2

—◇—

Please, God, Let Us Know
What We Are Doing

I was twenty-four when Nick and I got married, so basically an infant walking down the aisle. Please note: I'm sure there are many people who are fully mature and capable of making life decisions and life commitments and knowing what they are doing at the tender age of twenty-four, but I was not one of them. I'd graduated from college by the grace of something and found a job and started the process of dialing back my most egregious bad habits, but I still felt like someone playing at new life pretty much all of the time. It was a feeling that then I kept quiet because I thought I was alone in it, but later I would learn that a lot of us feel this way a whole lot of the time, and I think it's because very often our lives change before we do. Like there is this interim period where our insides need to catch up with our outsides and adjust to this new way of living, whether that is the big—and often positive—life changes like graduating from school or getting married or having a baby, or the other, harder things like losing someone we love or our marriage or our youth or pieces of ourselves.

So there I was in the in between, trying to get used to reporting to work at a time when before I had always still been tucked in bed sleeping something off, and I felt a little like the responsibility of all of it was going to kill me even though arguably my most serious responsibility after being home and on the couch in time for Thursday night Must See TV was keeping alive my cat, Zeke, and that should have been easy considering the way I was obsessed with him. Zeke had been the first thing I got for my first apartment on the first day I moved in, before I bought a bed or a set of dishes or any food for the fridge, and so I loved him in that annoying way that people who don't have kids love their pets. Most nights—and much to Nick's chagrin—Zeke slept on my pillow curled up around my head. The night before our wedding was the first night I'd ever spent away from the cat, and it also turned out to be the night he died. But I didn't know that when I walked down the aisle, not yet. There was a lot I didn't know.

Looking back, I'm pretty sure this is how it's supposed to work, that this is grace. I think we have to hold our noses and jump feet first into some of this stuff, even if it feels like we're faking it or bumbling around in it looking like a total fool. I had this conversation recently with a girlfriend who was contemplating a major life change, something she really wanted, except the time didn't feel exactly right. "Do you think it ever will?" I asked her, and after a minute she shook her head no, absorbing the weight of that reality. She just wanted to know for sure how it was going to turn out, she told me, and I wondered if she really did. Would any of us ever actually want to know what was swimming around in the water we were diving into? If I knew my beloved cat was going to die on my wedding day, would I have still brought him home with me to that little apartment? Further, if I knew how back-breakingly hard my marriage to Nick was going to be sometimes, the way he would challenge and frustrate and provoke me when we argued or we fell apart and how strange it would be to try to build a life together in partnership with someone after being raised by a single mother, would I have ever taken that first step down the aisle? I don't know the answers to those questions and I think that's on purpose. I think we aren't supposed to know, can't know, because to know *all* of it, to be able to see it laid out in front of us with its peaks and its valleys and the inevitable heartbreaks and growing pains, would make us so paralyzed with indecision that we'd never move, never start a new job or marry the person we love or commit to a new series on Netflix. So instead we leap, eyes and fists clenched tight against the terror, and we hope.

We were married on Valentine's Day, in a church that I'd always loved for its majesty yet somehow felt cavernous and overwhelming that February morning. Despite the considerable chill in the air, sweat pooled (attractively) on the inside of my wedding dress, and when I reached Nick at the end of the aisle I was yet again struggling to breathe. I grabbed both of his hands, leaned in close, and as everyone watched us greet each other I whispered to him the first romantic thing that occurred to me: "Did you remember to feed the cat?" It occurred to me that I was standing there in a poufy dress in front of everyone we loved about to marry a man I maybe didn't trust enough to feed my cat.

The cat, of course, was dead at this point. Nick had found him early that morning, curled up in an old cardboard toy box by the side of the road, frozen. We never knew for sure what happened, if he was hit by a car or how he even got out of the house, but Nick had spent the few hours before we had to be at the church driving around with Zeke's body in the trunk, looking for a vet open on Saturday mornings that could help. I, meanwhile, had spent the night at my mother's house and had no idea. A glimmer of something *must* have flashed across his face at my question, but my veil obstructed my view and I missed it.

The priest cleared his throat then, and I pushed all thoughts of the cat away as Nick and I and all of our collective expectations turned together to face him. My stomach flipped a little and the champagne I had downed in the limo despite my mother's look of stern disapproval (and the fact that it was technically still morning) threatened to make a reappearance. Was this really happening?

"We have gathered here together today to bring Elizabeth and Richard together in holy matrimony," the priest started in his thick accent.

"Nicholas," I whispered. "His name is *Nicholas*. Not Richard." But the priest didn't hear me or didn't care and I silently offered up the only prayer I prayed that day despite being in a church for a good chunk of time: "Please, God, let us know what we are doing."

I meant "us" in the sense of Nick and me, but I suppose I should have included the priest as well since he went on to call

Nick the wrong name the whole time, which was the kind of transgression you knew as it was happening that you'd laugh about, but not until later when it stopped seeming like a really big deal. He wasn't our priest, not the one with the kind face who we had met with after I'd worn my engagement ring around for two years and we decided maybe we should set an actual wedding date and Nick surprised me by insisting we get married in a church. "You mean like, in a *churchy* church? Like with a mass?" I'd asked, and so here we were, but without the kind-faced priest, who had broken the news to us a few weeks earlier—and after months of planning—that he was going to be vacationing in the tropics on our wedding day. He would have remembered Nick's name.

But we survived without him, and when his substitute pronounced Richard and me husband and wife and told Nick to kiss the bride, the relief that I had lived through the ceremony was so palpable that my hand shot out towards the congregation in a thumbs-up sign, of all things. We made it, my thumb signaled, and all those people out there who loved us laughed a little too hard probably because they had seen how my nervousness was shining off me in hot waves of champagne and perspiration. We made it, I thought to myself as we walked back down that aisle together now, husband and wife, which is hilarious because the truth is we had only just begun.

I think about that prayer now and I'm so grateful that God was smart enough not to answer it. Because I can tell you unequivocally now that we did not, in fact, know what we were doing. Of course we didn't. How can you know? How could I have had any idea the magnitude of ways we would change and shift and struggle and grow, both together and separately?

I think God knew what I didn't, which was that I needed a little bit of protective ignorance in order to safely make it down that aisle and back, the same way it was good that I didn't know how hard pregnancy was, or how much giving birth would hurt, or the ways in which being a mother would rip me apart and put me back together unrecognizable to my former self. And had I known, the overwhelming-ness of it all likely would have completely paralyzed me. I think I'd still be standing there sweating my ass off in the cold church, trying to find the perfect time to walk into the next chapter. And for all of the magic that came later that I would have missed out on, believe me when I say: sometimes it's better not to know what we are doing at all.

———◊———

I thought again of this prayer many years later when, for no particular reason other than I was having a rough day, I did what any normal person would do: I dug my wedding dress out of the attic and wore it while I made dinner. It barely fit, four pregnancies having changed my body in ways that would have terrified all of the innocence right out of twenty-four-year-old-blushing-bride-me. Thanks to all of that exuberant drinking and dancing we did late into the night on that fateful Valentine's Day in 2004, the dress was also covered in wine stains and missing half of its buttons, and yet it still made me feel pretty in a way that my regular evening uniform of bleach stained yoga pants couldn't match. Maybe more importantly, it got me thinking of that younger version of me who wore this dress so earnestly all of those years ago, walking out of that church with the courage only naivete and late morning champagne can provide.

And what if she *had* known? What would the me-then have thought of the me-now, or of this life that I live so messily and love so much and fail so often at? Would she be proud? I'm guessing she'd be a little embarrassed of me in much the same way that I am of her, mostly because she was so incredibly unprepared for all of the huge ways her life was going to change in the next decade, but also because she got pretty dang buzzed up that night and danced like a total fool. I wonder too what I would I say to that hopeful blushing bride with her singular and silly prayer: Please, God let us know what we are doing. I guess I could tell her the truth: Girl, you have no idea what you're doing.

Walking down the aisle is the easy part. Tonight you will celebrate—as you should—drinking, eating, drinking some more, and then dancing so fiercely that your mom will pull you aside and quietly remind you, "Elizabeth, your grandmother is here." Tomorrow you will have a headache and a wedding band and a plane trip to Key West to pack for where you will sip more drinks on a big boat and wax philosophical about the perfect kids you will have and the dizzying career heights you will achieve. Your collective future will spread out in front of you both like an open book and it likely will be the biggest turning point of your whole life.

And then you will come home and make babies and have babies and instead of an open book, life will now seem to stretch out in front of you like one long painful nursing session and your new husband and you will yell at each other in the middle of the night with bags under your eyes that you are still much too young to have about whose turn it is to get the baby, *again*. Your cushion of protective ignorance that carried you down the aisle will be replaced with the absolutely crippling anxiety of new motherhood, and you and your marriage will spend long, uncomfortable periods of time teetering on the precipice of not-gonna-make-it.

But you will make it. And you will fall so incredibly, deeply in love with your babies that it will make you fall in love all over again with your husband. The two of you will make this magical life in a big old creaky house filled with way too many throw pillows that feels like home in a way that nothing else ever has, and you will learn to sleep in a big king-sized bed with four kids in between you and still, somehow, touch.

Still, you should know too that you will break—and often— because having this family is like walking around with five open wounds that make you more vulnerable than you ever were before. You'll find God in a whole new way and pray feverishly that you all stay protected, and of course, you don't. You will ache and fall on your knees with the force of it and be absolutely, completely convinced that you can never get up again.

And then you will get back up.

You will change diapers and do laundry and make and buy and clean up food until it feels like you do nothing else, and you will go to your therapist (because yes, you will have a therapist) and say, "What is the point of all of this?" and he, a grey-haired poet who you would be at a dangerous risk of falling in love with if he didn't insist on talking about feelings all the damn time will say, "The Buddha would say: chop wood, carry water. So maybe for you, it's change diaper, make mac and cheese." And you will go home that night and after everyone falls asleep and the house is blissfully silent, you will suddenly burst out laughing because you totally get it.

And years from now—if you are really, really lucky—you will stand in your kitchen in an old wedding dress, you and your rock of a husband, the island in the swirling chaos of children around you, and he will say to you, "Honey, this mac and cheese is amazing," and even though you know he's lying because it came out of a box and is made from orange powder, you'll take the compliment because that's what you do for each other.

"Thanks, Babe. It must be the dress."

"Oh, are you wearing a dress?" he'll say. "I didn't even notice."

Except of course the truest truth is I probably shouldn't tell her anything at all, because no words would ever be able to do justice to the real truth, which is that if we knew exactly what we were leaping into we'd suck all of the glorious magic right out of it. And what a loss that would be in the end.

———◊———

The morning after the wedding I woke up to see that Nick was watching me. I rolled over to face him, my head—still pounding from the revelry of the reception—protesting the sudden movement. "Hey, Babe, do you think we are even legally married? Or maybe I am married to someone named Richard?"

This time I saw the something that flashed across Nick's face. "I have to tell you something," he said.

"I hope it's that he's wildly rich," I said, dragging myself up in search of coffee. "Get it? *Rich*?"

But he didn't laugh. "Liz? Zeke died."

"Wait, what? When?" All sorts of things flashed through my head, but mostly I remembered how Nick had been waiting for me at the end of what felt like the longest church aisle in the world yesterday and when I got next to him, finally, the only stupid thing I was able to think of to say had been, "Did you feed the cat?"

And then I thought of how they say you should be able to keep alive a plant before you have a pet, and then you should keep a pet alive before you even think about having a relationship, and here I had a shiny new marriage but no pet anymore because he had died on my wedding day and I don't know what exactly they say about that, but I bet it's that everything was doomed.

"Why didn't you tell me yesterday?" I asked. My first instinct was to be deeply embarrassed that I hadn't known, that I had danced and carried on and celebrated while there was a sadness just around the corner, waiting.

"I don't know. It was our wedding day," he said. "I wanted you to be happy." And gosh had I been, at least from the thumbs up onward. A little too happy, maybe, but here it was again: if I had known the truth, the whole truth about what lay ahead for me the next morning, the immense pain that now sat hot in my gut from losing the first pet I'd ever had, how would I ever have made it through what was then the biggest day of my adult life? Would I have ever been able to enjoy it? I'd prayed for knowledge, for security and promises and truth, and yet the thing that had probably saved my wedding day was what had been kept from me.

The next day we left for our honeymoon on a plane so small it looked like something you could buy in the toy aisle at Target. We hit some turbulence, and Nick grabbed my hand and I kept holding onto him long after the plane settled, trying to keep my grief quiet. An elderly man shuffled slowly past us then on his way to the airplane bathroom and stopped when he recognized us. It was our priest—the one we had wanted, the one with the kind face—on his way to the tropics.

"Elizabeth. Nicholas. Congratulations and God bless you," he said, touching each of us on the shoulder before he made his way back down the aisle.

"Well I suppose now it's official," I said to Nick after the priest walked away. "I hope we can break the news to Richard gently."

Nick leaned in close. "Can I ask you something? Why did everyone laugh when we were pronounced husband and wife? Did I do something wrong?"

He hadn't seen my thumbs up, I realized. He hadn't known. And I thought about how while I was doing my makeup and downing champagne, he had spent the morning of our wedding running around trying to find a veterinarian's office open on a Saturday to cremate a cat he didn't even particularly like, and then held onto the secret to protect me while I danced and drank many more glasses of champagne. How he had done the best he could with what he knew and figured the rest out as he went along, which—combined with enough blind faith to keep on taking the next step—might be the best recipe for a successful marriage I could think of.

"Oh, no," I said, squeezing his hand. "You did everything right." And I turned back towards the window to watch as we floated over the clouds, wondering if I could spot Zeke fly by on his way to cat heaven, thinking maybe we weren't doomed after all.

3

———◇———

Objects in the Mirror

When my belly was just starting to swell for the very first time with our very first baby, Nick and I moved our assortment of beer-ring-stained Target furniture and mismatched hand-me-downs into our first real home. Despite it being a total fixer upper, despite the previous owner's extremely question-able paint color choices, and despite feeling like I was going to throw up pretty much constantly—because of the baby, not the paint choices—it was probably the most exciting moment of my life. Everything felt so, well, pregnant with possibility. We were newly married, we had new jobs, we had a new house and soon, a new baby. After a rocky start, my life seemed to stretch right out in front of me like a fresh, clean slate. I couldn't wait.

We scheduled moving day for a Saturday and enlisted the help of anyone who would accept beer and pizza as a legit form of payment (this is a surprisingly small list, by the way, because moving is the literal worst), but the Friday evening before I was completely unable to contain myself any longer and went over to the new house while Nick was at work. I brought some of the lighter things I could actually carry over there with me—kitchen appliances and some of my clothes—but really all I wanted to do was stand in the middle of all that wide open possibility, hold my little belly, and dream.

When I got tired of calling out profanity in the empty cavernous rooms just to hear my own echoes, I dragged the clothes I had brought over—pretty things on hangers that had no chance of fitting me for many, many months—up to what would be our master bedroom. The room was dusty and outdated and covered in floor to ceiling wallpaper that had to be older than I was and looked it, yellow where it should have been white and peeling away from the wall in the corners, but the evening light flooded in through the curtainless windows just the same and the pieces of the room seemed to add themselves up into something much more beautiful than the actual sum of their parts. "We are going to make a life here," I thought.

There were two closets in the room and I assumed they were identical until I opened them and realized only one of the two had a full-length mirror hung on the inside of the door. I stood there in between the two doors until the hangers started to dig into my hands, looking at myself in that mirror and feeling all my previous excitement drain out of my body. I was sweaty and my hair was stuck to my forehead in places and sticking up in others. I was a couple months pregnant and fat in all the wrong places: my face and my butt and already, somehow, my ankles. My belly stuck out but just a little, giving me the silhouette of a large flesh-colored rectangle. Nothing fit right, my freckles were out in full force, and I had a pimple or three. Of course now I can look back and see how, like the room, all those separate pieces of me could and did add up to something more beautiful than the sum of my parts, but then all I saw was a list of flaws.

So slowly and carefully, I shut the door of the closet with the mirror. And then I hung my pretty little clothes that wouldn't fit me for many, many months (or more likely, ever again) in the other closet, the one without the mirror. Nick looked at me questioningly the next day when he realized which one I'd claimed, but I just shrugged. I didn't lie, but I didn't tell him the truth either: I didn't want to have to look at myself every time I opened my closet door.

By then the active part of my eating disorder was behind me and had been for many years, but I'd never really been able to pull myself out of that place of self-criticism, and being pregnant had challenged me in a whole new way. Every morning I would wake up to something new and different going on with my body: the belly, sure, but also the swelling and the stretch marks and the hemorrhoids and the bone-deep fatigue, to name a few. It all felt very out of my control—because of course, it was out of my control—and considering eating disorders tend to be about control, I knew I had to be careful.

So I chose the closet without the mirror, thinking I was doing myself a favor but unable to ignore the tug of worry in my heart, the voice that kept asking what kind of lessons was someone like me, someone still not totally able to look herself square in the mirror, going to teach her future children? I agonized over this, tracing and retracing my steps in my own life and trying to pinpoint when it had gone wrong, when I had learned what so many of us did as girls: that people would like us better if we pruned and primped and shrunk ourselves to fit what society expected of our bodies, our personalities, our dreams. My own mother was a working mom and a feminist, yet every day I watched her criticize herself for things that had nothing to do with her ability and everything to do with what she looked like. I can still picture her–beautiful by anyone's standards yet completely unaware of it–staring into her mirror with a look of total disgust, me and my sister underfoot and watching. The lesson was that while we may be able to do anything–fight the patriarchy and bust through the glass ceiling and demand equal pay for equal work and paid family leave and the rights to do whatever with our bodies that we wish–we damn well better look good while we do it.

My own eating disorder had begun with a friendly diet competition between my mother and myself, each of us trying to drop five pounds to look better in a bathing suit. It had started lighthearted and innocently enough–as innocent as denying yourself sustenance can be, that is–until I'd been unable to stop, something in me latching onto that restriction in a way that I'd assume other addicts latch onto their drug of choice. Eventually I'd lost fifty pounds and my period and my hair, and I needed help or I was going to die.

Very few places had dedicated eating disorder clinics in the late nineties, so what that help looked like was me and an older and alarmingly skinny woman named Tina sharing a room and a treatment plan as the only two anorexics in a general psychiatric facility. I was only seventeen years old, and Tina's mere existence as an older woman with an eating disorder felt like a warning to me. Each night of the handful I lasted in the clinic I would wake up in the early morning hours before the sun to the ragged sound of Tina's quick breath as she did thousands of stolen sit-ups in the dark (exercise, while encouraged for everyone else in the facility, was forbidden to us). The two of us never had a soul-baring conversation but I felt like I knew her well enough anyway, maybe because in some basic way she reminded me of my mother, or maybe because there's a special kind of intimacy that comes with being forced to document each other's trips to the bathroom. Either way it felt like Tina was the ghost of my anorexia future, a specter that came in the night and warned me of all that could be if I didn't get my shit together soon. Being her age felt a whole universe away to me then, and the mere suggestion that I could be like her—that I could carry my eating disorder with me well into my womanhood—was terrifying.

It was only later, when the years had softened both my body and my disease, that I realized what I had recognized of my mother in Tina. It was the look on her face when she looked at herself, that sad resignation of never-going-to-be-good-enough perfectionism that had long ago ensured in each woman's life that every single glance in a mirror was inevitably going to disappoint. It's the same look I saw on my own face that first night in our new house, and that—the prospect of teaching my own children what had been taught to me—scared me more than any pimple or cankles or hemorrhoids ever could. I pictured them watching me standing there in front of this closet, staring at the list of flaws the mirror had served up, adjusting and fixing and judging myself the same way I had watched my mother (and Tina) look at herself. *Not again*, I said to myself. Not my babies.

So when I hung my clothes in the other closet, arrogantly thinking I could break the cycle of generations of women before me simply by picking a closet without a mirror, it was in part to save me from myself but maybe also to save them too. Because this was something I'd wrestled with ever since I'd peed on the stick and saw those two pink lines: How do I, healing but not healed, teach these babies to properly love themselves? I was in recovery but that didn't mean I was whole or ever would be again. A few years of starvation had left me with permanent damage to my body. My hunger and satiety signals would never again function the way a healthy person's do, and food forever for me would be imbued with meaning well beyond fuel. Sometimes I still forget to eat because my body forgets to remind me, and other times I forget to stop, and I always have to watch myself to make sure I'm not dancing on the edge of something dangerous like falling back into deprivation. I'd lay awake at night and pray,

> God, help me teach them what I may not totally know myself: to be strong, to love themselves, to do normal stuff like eat when they are hungry and stop when they are full and move in their bodies because it feels good and not because they want to target a trouble zone. Help me close the loop that my mother started when she sat me down and taught me that we could do anything we put our minds to, because she was right, we can, and that's so important. What's not important, not even a little bit, is how we look while we do it.

Except of course I haven't had to teach them any of this, not once, not yet. In what is probably the most ordinary miracle of all, they were born and just inherently knew. They came out hungry for life, instinctively wanting to move and fighting to learn how. They're older now and still haven't stopped moving, not once, not even when I ask them to because we're in church or it's bedtime. And I know too that they're not doing it so they can justify that second scoop of ice cream because how ridiculous is that; to them ice cream is just that, ice cream. It isn't love and naughtiness and wounds and numbness and something they will have guilt over eating long after the taste has faded from their mouths, because while these are my babies, they are not me.

———◊———

I was driving a while back with my daughter Gabby in the car while she yelled her fool head off at me from the backseat.

"Mommy! Look!"

"Honey, I'm driving," I told her. "I will look in a sec." I thought about also explaining that she doesn't need to yell, since the space between her mouth and the back of my head was at max, eight inches, but math wasn't her forte yet, and I hadn't had enough coffee to engage that much.

"Mommy, look." All sorts of things that she could want me to see ran through my head, a ticker tape of possible motherhood horrors. She'd puked. She'd peed. She'd pooped. She'd blown her nose down her shirt. She'd opened the window and thrown her pants/shirt/little brother out of it. We reached a stop sign—thank God—and I turned around enough in my seat to see that it wasn't any of those things. It was her belly. She was holding up her shirt, pointing. "Look at my belly! Isn't it great?"

And so I did. I looked. I idled at that stop sign for a second and I looked at her like I hadn't in a while, took in her curls unbrushed and her bare feet hopelessly dirty, her too-tight shirt not quite long enough to cover that belly even if she wasn't holding it up. Her face was tilted up towards me, and I saw the lesson in it plainly, how I'd had it wrong before. I've watched in humbled awe as each one of my children, born whole, just inherently knew the things I prayed over having to teach, and I think now that my job here as their mother isn't to teach them to love themselves, but rather to help them hold as tight as they can to the natural love they were born knowing. Maybe to mother is less to mold as it is to soften the blows of the universe and keep these babies alive and eager and from closing up tight around their wounds the way I had, the way my mother before me had, the way so many of us have, getting bitter and hard in the very places where we used to be wide-eyed and soft.

These are the things they don't tell you about motherhood. How after a lifetime of struggling to love yourself it will be an absolute miracle to love these babies so wholly and unconditionally, sure. But also how they will love themselves the same way, at least at first, and in that maybe you will find a level of healing that all the therapy and self-help in the world couldn't get you to because you will realize at some point you must have loved yourself the very same way. Or how seeing the way they are so comfortable in their own skin, the way they strut around so confident in the fact that they are the masterpiece we too believe them to be, will make all the work we've done trying to suck it all in or hide it or simply avoid looking at it in the mirror seem kind of silly. Because of course it is. It's against everything we were born knowing.

———◊———

A few weeks after Gabby showed me her belly, I was alone in my room changing my clothes, and there in the corner was my mirror. By now, we live in a different and bigger house and I have a different and bigger body, but me and this mirror are still slowly working it out. So I stood there in front of it for a while, sucking my belly in and letting it back out, looking at my stretch marks and my cellulite, my less-than-perky breasts. My list of flaws is definitely longer now than it was when I was younger, if we're still keeping track, and the truth is trying not to fall back into that dangerous pattern still takes work.

And I don't think I'm alone in that, nor do I think its limited to people who are in recovery from eating disorders. I've talked to a lot of women of all shapes and sizes with all sorts of bodies and stories and lives who, like me, still sometimes need to be reminded of what we once all must have instinctively known: that each of us put together is a total so very much more than a sum of our individual parts. I think it's just that our filter—the normal part of us that is essential to being a woman in today's world, the part that reminds us on the daily how in the grand scheme of things worth has little to do with pants size or makeup or what any of us looks like and much more to do with what we are—can get a teensy bit broken.

Broken is probably not even the right word for it; it's more like it's running low on juice and needs to be charged. It's still sending up little reminders to us, but instead of the loud and incessant alarm necessary to drown out all the other noise, they're quiet chirps like the smoke alarm on its last legs, easy to ignore and probably just as dangerous. So sometimes when I stand in front of my mirror in the morning and nurse my coffee, the chirps get lost in the chorus of self-doubt, a pool that's deep enough for any of us to drown in if we're not being careful.

Because that's the thing, isn't it? We have to actively be careful not to let that junk kill us. We have to walk around with our eyes wide open and notice the actual beauty of our lives, the things that matter, or we risk getting incessantly stuck in the call of the things that don't. We risk throwing all of our money and time and effort after the crap that TV and magazine covers and every air-brushed image that floats past our eyeballs a hundred times a day tells us is important that really isn't important at all, at least not the kind of important that matters when the lights go out, or when the years go by, or when we are feeling a little fragile and sad and need help. Which is, of course, when we need to be reminded the most.

So if, like me, you need it, here's the reminder: we were created and born with every bit of the self-love we need to get through each and every morning when the blanket of darkness is so heavy that we aren't sure we are going to be able to breathe much longer underneath the weight of it. I saw the proof this everywhere in this life, once I started paying attention. It's in the hugs of a hundred kids on a hundred nights, the little ones who fall asleep against my belly, still soft from them, and the bigger ones too who pad in after I've started to fall asleep and bend towards me just enough, the way a plant will bend slightly towards the sun, and whisper so quiet I will doubt it happened at all, "I love you." It's the unbrushed curls and the dirty feet and the belly full of milk I warmed of a child who is so, so much more things than the sum of her parts. It's the way they love themselves wholly and unabashedly, which is the same way we love them and the same way God loves us and the same way we are meant to love ourselves. It's the way all of us were born whole, madly in love with ourselves just as we should be, before the wounds of a lifetime of bad messages crept in and drowned out the chirping reminders.

Just then the girls tumbled into my room as they do, loudly and without warning or knocking. Gabby ran right up to me, grabbed a fistful of my stomach, and said, "Mommy, you have a great belly too."

And slowly, still half naked with my belly gripped in my daughter's sticky hand, I made myself stop sucking it in. It felt unnatural at first and then it felt vulnerable and then it felt like exhaling a breath I had been holding since puberty. It felt, finally, like freedom.

4

—◊—

Trapped in the Elevator

When I was thirty-six weeks pregnant with my youngest son, I almost died.

All right, I'm being a little dramatic. I didn't exactly *almost die*. But for a second late one afternoon on my way home from work, I did think I was about to die, and that should count for something here in this story I'm about to tell you.

My office then was on the fifteenth floor of a downtown high-rise and empty by the time I left. I stepped into the elevator and pressed the button for the ground floor, but we only dropped a foot or two before the machinery made an awful metal-on-metal crunching noise and stopped.

Note that it's important you know this is *not* actually when I thought I was dying. In fact, I was still only paying half attention to what was going on at this point, thinking about what we could have for dinner that required the least amount of actual effort and chewing away on my fingernail, a habit I'd had since I was a kid despite my mother's best efforts to stop me. When I realized we had stopped moving, I nonchalantly pressed the Open Door button on the elevator's control panel with the hand that wasn't in my mouth. No big deal. This wasn't my first rodeo, you see. I had been stuck in the elevator before, even had to use the intercom call button to ask for help, which had looked like this, that first time:

Intercom Guy: "Yello?"

Me: "I'm stuck in the elevator."

Intercom Guy: [Silence. Possible chewing noises.]

Me: "Hello? Stuck in elevator here?"

Intercom Guy: "Yeah, um, have you tried pressing the button labeled Open Door?

Me: [Silence. Presses "Open Door" button. Doors slide open. Embarrassingly sneaks out of elevator.]

Intercom Guy: [Quiet in the distance now as I walked away.] "Yello?"

Except this time, pressing the Open Door button had no effect at all, and just for good measure I tried reverse psychology and pressed the Close Door button, which also did not open the door. This was when I started to pay a little bit of attention. I had places to be and mouths to feed (chief among them, mine), and was at the stage of pregnancy where I needed to pee approximately every three minutes or so. Being stuck was not something that was going to fit conveniently into my life, not at that moment.

But when the elevator car dropped out from under me suddenly, the force of the fall throwing me off-balance and into the back wall—hard—that was when I *really* started to pay attention.

My finger was still in my mouth when I fell and I bit down on it accidentally. The pain of that mixed with my surprise and fear made me gasp and then mew this weird guttural nonword that sounded a lot like "Mom," because no matter how screwed up your situation with your mother is you will still call out for her when you think you are dying, trust me.

And we were pretty screwed up at that point, my mother and me, but it hadn't always been that way either. When I was a little girl, I absolutely adored my mother. It seemed easy to love her then, maybe because of the optimism of childhood or maybe because she didn't drink that much yet, or not that we saw, anyway. In restaurants she would order a glass of white wine and leave it mostly untouched, looking past it the same way she looked past most temptations, especially those with calories. Or maybe it was because everyone else loved her too, the mailmen and the handymen and each one of her four husbands, sure, but also anyone lucky enough to be in the same place at the same time with her. She would smile at you and it was like you had been given a gift that you would then spend the rest of your life chasing. Kind of like heroin.

I don't know when any of that shifted, really, and whether it was a gradual descent into the depth of the hole her and I ended up in or if it had happened all at once. What I do know is that I spent years trying arrogantly to fix it all, staging catastrophic interventions that no one wanted to come to and pouring out whatever liquor bottles I could find. I sucked up false promises like an overeager child. There wasn't any contempt in me then, not at first anyway, just sadness and pain and a growing sense of helplessness. But a decade of disappointments and lies went by, and eventually I'd cycled through every possible emotion and ended up numb with it all, slowly distancing myself from the first relationship I ever had with the most tentative of baby steps, feigning a callousness and strength that I was never really sure I actually had in me at all because it was the only way I knew how to protect myself and my kids.

But the truth that I tried to pretend away was apparent in that one nonword *mew*. I missed my mother something fierce. And missing your mother—whether she is alive or not—is an ache that lives deeply ingrained in the core of your being, in the primal pace that regulates the most basic things like breath and heartbeat and my love for my children and the way I think mushrooms and cheeseburgers and a good Cabernet are the most delicious things in the world. I missed her then even though she was still alive, even if she wasn't all the way gone yet, because she wasn't there either, not really. She wasn't there in the way I thought a mother should be or could be and certainly not in the way she had been for us before. So I missed her in that nasally, whiny, victim-y way, where if I had been able to talk about it plainly (I wasn't, it was forbidden), I would have been pretty insufferable to listen to and after about two seconds you would have wanted to stab me in the eyeball with your finger just to get me to please shut up.

I even missed made-up stuff that wasn't even real, like the wisdom I wanted her to give me when I was standing in a swaying empty elevator car carrying thirty (forty) extra pregnancy pounds and a crazed, manic shining across my face. I wanted her to be able to say "you're going to get out of here, don't worry" to me like this broken elevator car was no big thing at all and for me to believe it because maybe she'd get out of where she was trapped too and become a happy, normal, everyday kind of grandma who wore floppy hats and worked in a garden and kept her house decorated in the smudges of my children's fingerprints instead of hidden, empty vodka bottles.

And then I laughed, out loud and a little maniacally, because all I could picture her saying if she *was* there was, "I told you to stop biting your fucking fingernails and get your shit together, Elizabeth," and I don't know, but maybe in some ways she was always with me no matter what.

I pressed my forehead against the cold metal of the elevator wall, shook my hand until my finger stopped throbbing so much, and then made my way back to front of the elevator car where the emergency intercom button was glowing bright like a beacon. I pressed that thing like it was my epidural pump in labor, and thought quickly: Shit. I hope Yello Guy doesn't remember me.

But it wasn't Yello Guy. It was a soft, gentle voice, and it piped in from the speaker and filled the elevator car. "Are you okay?"

"I think I might be stuck," I said. "I even pressed the Open Door button. I swear."

Then he said the exact right thing, the thing I'd wished my mother would have said. "You're going to get out of here, don't worry." And for a second, in the dimly lit elevator car that I swear was rocking gently side to side, with this kind, paternal voice booming in overhead, I wondered if I had actually died and this was what it was like to walk into the light.

I remembered then how when I was young, little still, I used to sometimes roll off my bed in my sleep. I think this is actually pretty common, and it's probably why they make those guard rails now that my own kids had when they were around that same age. And it wasn't usually that big of a deal.

I would wake up when I hit the floor—which thankfully was carpeted—shake the dust from my hair and climb back into my bed. No one else even needed to know, thank you very much, because I was embarrassed and proud and desperately wanted to be more grown up than I actually was. Everything was fine.

That is, of course, until it wasn't.

Until one night I rolled off the bed and this time, I didn't wake up. Instead I kept right on rolling, somehow ending up fully underneath my own bed where I must have slept for a while like a total freak. And when I did wake up a little while later, it was to complete terror and confusion because I had no idea where I was. I tried to sit up, only to hit my head against the underside of the mattress. I can still feel the claustrophobia of it all, the sensation of being trapped and alone in the dark, the realization that I was in a situation I did not know how to get myself out of.

So I did what anyone would do, what my instinct still had me doing as an adult swinging in a free-falling elevator. I called for my mother. My voice must have been muffled by the mattress and the bedding but somehow she'd heard me anyway and came running into my room, confused at first and then a little scared when she didn't see me anywhere. She didn't know about how I'd been falling out of my bed because I hadn't told her, of course. So it took the two of us calling out to each other, a late night mother-daughter freaked out version of Marco Polo, for me to be found and eventually pulled to my rescue. Afterwards, once I was safely back in her arms and back in my bed, both of us were reduced to the kind of spontaneous giggling fits that seem to only happen when you think you're doomed and then you realize you're still alive and everything is okay and all of it, all that primal terror and confusion, just seems funny in retrospect.

I'd been quiet for too long, sucked into my memories. "Are you okay?" the intercom voice asked me again, and wasn't that the question, right there? Was I okay? I was thirty-three years old and a mother of three and I might have just wet myself a little, and my belly was so full with yet another baby that I was constantly surprised by the fact that I could still move around at will at all. My fingers had been swollen like sausages for months and now one of them was bleeding, slowly, dripping a little on the elevator floor. My mother and I were so screwed up and I was so mad at her most of the time that I couldn't think straight except apparently I still mewed her name when I got scared. But also, I had thought for a second I was plummeting to my death and then I didn't, miracle of miracles, thanks be to God or Jesus or just plain luck.

So I told him I was okay. And the baby kicked and my belly shook and I wondered what the odds were that I would give birth right there on the elevator floor. By this time I'd been having contractions on and off for weeks, which they told me was normal when it's your hundredth baby but I was never sure I believed them all of the way. Something in me was completely convinced this one would come in a special way or maybe just fall out while I was doing the dishes one night, and with the dim light of the elevator, the quiet space, and God-voice on the mic: there were worse places to give birth.

But my baby didn't come then. The firemen did, breaking my reverie with their loud boot steps, knocking on the elevator doors and shouting down to me. My legs had fallen asleep underneath my heavy belly and I struggled to stand up again.

"Miss," they called to me through the door, and I loved them then too for calling me *Miss* and not *Ma'am*. (It's easy to love people when you almost die and then don't.) "The elevator door is jammed shut, so we are going to force it open using a crowbar. Please back away from the door."

I obliged, backed away. God-voice asked me if I was still okay, but it was too loud to answer through the noise of the doors being wrenched open with a crowbar, metal on metal again but not as scary this time. Slowly the doors started to open and light flooded in from above along with the gentle faces on the firemen. I blinked slowly, my eyes trying to adjust to the bright again.

The car had fallen and then stuck in between floors, and one of the firemen jumped down into the car and dropped to his knee. "Miss," he started, and it was even better this time that he chose *Miss* because he could actually see me now, eight months huge and ruddy-faced. "I would like you step up onto my knee. My partner up there will reach down and grab you and pull you up into the lobby."

I looked at him, and at his partner. Then I looked down at my belly, and finally at my shoes, heavy wooden clogs. "You want me to step on you?" I asked. I had never felt larger.

"Miss, I need you to step on me in order for me to rescue you."

"Um, I am wearing very heavy shoes," I said, pointing to my feet.

"And I am a firefighter," he countered, pointing to his uniform.

And so I stepped, and he held me, lifted me up even, and his partner pulled me to safety the same way my mother had pulled me out from under the bed and into the light all those years ago. And while it wasn't exactly a graceful rising and somehow my skirt twisted so bad around me that the maternity panel ended up supporting my butt for a while instead of my belly, I still ended up standing on solid ground.

"Miss, are you okay?"

I'm not sure who even asked this the last time, either a firefighter or God again or all of them together in three-part harmony, but when I said, "I'm okay," I meant it, even twirled a little in my backwards skirt as I walked away.

A couple of days later, my mom called me. We hadn't been okay for so long and I usually wouldn't even have answered but I think it was what happened in the elevator that made me pick up that time. "Yello?" I said, tentatively.

"Honey! I heard you got stuck in an elevator," she said, and instead of an argument she was just my mom again for this moment. "Are you okay?"

"I am, Mom," I answered. "I'm okay." And I was.

I didn't know it then, of course, but it was the last conversation we ever had. She died a few days later, and in the first chaotic weeks of grief I thought of that elevator and how quickly everything can change: you can be just standing still all minding your own business when the floor drops out from under you and you're thrown right off your feet. It's completely terrifying and it's easy then to get stuck in unfamiliar territory, where the only way out is going to be calling out Marco and trusting, even while your heart tries to gallop right out of your chest, that the Polo is coming. And *it is*. There are people who will quite literally lift you up, grab your hands and pull. It's happened before and it will happen again, of this I am sure, as long as I continue to have the faith to call out.

5

———◇———

Sometimes Just Breathing Is a Victory

Something in me shifted the day my mother died. When my sister called to tell me, I was sitting in my car in the parking garage, getting ready to leave work. "It's Mom," my sister said. "She's gone."

"What does that mean?" I asked, not quite paying attention, not quite comprehending. "She's gone? Gone where?"

"She died, Liz. She's dead. Mom's dead."

While it wasn't what I had expected to hear, wasn't the normal "she's in the hospital" or "she's drunk" that usually opened an "it's Mom" conversation, I can't say that I was surprised, not really. My mother had been drinking herself into catatonic states for at least a decade, and I had been waiting for this phone call for almost as long, had rehearsed this whole scene in my head countless times. I knew just how it would go: I would sink to the ground, overcome with grief. I'd crumple. I'd weep. I'd wail. I have a friend who uses the expression *kneed* to describe the effect that something so big and emotional and heavy has on you when you first hear it and you are, quite literally, knocked to your knees, and I had always known that when this time did come, when my mother was finally gone, I would be instantly kneed. Except none of that happened.

I wasn't kneed, not then anyway, and not just because I was already sitting or even because I was so pregnant that had I fallen to my knees, the likelihood of me giving birth right there on the dirty parking garage floor went up much higher than I was willing to risk. What happened instead was I told my sister to shut the fuck up, not once but three times, and then I forgot how to breathe. I'm still not sure how this happened, how someone could possibly forget how to do a basic and innate thing such as breathe. The breath had gone in okay, sucked hard into my lungs when the full meaning of what she said hit me. But try as I might, I could not get my body to exhale it back out again.

Everything in my vision turned red. Sweat started to run in rivulets down my back and I heard my heart drumming in my ears, but for the life of me I couldn't remember how to exhale. The car was warm from sitting in the sun all day—it was September but the weather was like summer still—and the steering wheel was hot enough that later I'd find a mark on my pregnant belly where I'd pressed up against it, trying not to pass out.

I looked up then, and at my side was a woman staring at me, hands pressed to the window of my car, mouthing "are you okay?" when I met her gaze. She was close enough to the window that when she spoke her own breath left a small oval of condensation on the glass, and I watched it, mesmerized as it grew smaller and faded in front of me. It was exactly what I needed, her reminder of breath, and I exhaled my stuck hot stale air all at once and with enough force to lift a sweaty curl from the middle of my forehead.

"There once was a girl, who had a little curl, right in the middle of her forehead," went the rhyme my mother used to sing to me while brushing my hair.

And this exhalation, my sweet friends, was a victory. It doesn't sound like much, I know, and it probably usually isn't. Breathing is maybe the single most important thing we do all day long, and yet how often is it in the forefront of our minds? How often do we find ourselves in a situation where we are reminded of the absolute sweet miracle that is fresh air moving in and out of our own bodies? And yes, I know, it sounds silly. It was. I'd had thirty-three years of experience with breathing already, and for all of that time before it had come easily and without a second thought. But this was a new time.

And again I'd been asked the question, was I okay? I'm sure she thought I was in labor; there was no way she could have known that my mother had hung herself that morning and she'd just been found, that my sister had called to tell me and I'd told her to shut the fuck up again and again until she asked me to please, for the love of all that is sacred, stop saying that. So while technically the answer to the good Samaritan's question was probably no, everything was not okay and maybe never was going to be again, there was also the truth that I was breathing now, and maybe that was okay enough, at least for now. I nodded at her and tried to make my eyes look soft, and she walked away after a good long minute of looking me searchingly in the face, never knowing how she probably saved my life. I felt a sense of calm descend over me, grateful for every successful exhale that left my lips.

Maybe this new perspective was just adrenaline; I don't know, I'm not a scientist. Maybe it's something that God gives us so we don't absolutely shatter into a thousand pieces under the blows that a life can render. Or maybe there's a reframing that comes with tragedy that is kind of like when you step out into the natural sunlight for the first time all day after being inside in a climate-controlled, artificially lit building and everything looks the way it should for a second: so bright and so dazzling and so colorful that it hurts to stare directly at it for too long. Either way, I figured it was temporary and I'd forget soon enough to be grateful for each breath, later that night or in the chaos of the next few days while we went through the motions of planning a funeral for the woman who held me while my lungs took their first gulps of air.

But I haven't forgotten, not entirely. My mother killed herself and I fell apart in the aftermath in a thousand different ugly and unglamorous ways, but I held onto that realization with a white-knuckled death grip because I knew it was powerful enough to save me when I found myself alone in the dark again. If you looked in my hand right now, five years later, you would see me hanging onto it still. It is my lifeline.

And it changes things.

I drove home from the parking garage after hanging up with my sister, and it was like I could finally see. Life is funny like that, I suppose, not ha-ha funny but deep, painful, ironic funny, in that someone else's death can pull you out of your own life and make you stop, blink, think. Wait. Was all this beauty here all along? Loss changes things. Surviving changes things. Finding yourself alone in the dark and then managing to pull yourself out, whether alone or by the grace of God or by the grace of a stranger in the car window reminding you how to exhale, changes things. It's a turn of events I'd wish on no one, ever, and yet it's a turn of events we probably will all experience in some form at some point, and when we do it's real hard not to come out of that dark night different than we were when we went in. I drove and the sun was brilliantly yellow and the trees were green and the breeze came in gentle from the window, and it wasn't exactly pleasant; of course not, I was twisted up in shock now and aching, but I was breathing and I was seeing and I was noticing for the first time in a long time. And that was enough to get me home.

Nick stepped out into the sunshine of the front porch as I climbed up the stairs, heavy with the carrying of myself, our unborn baby, my Tupperware from lunch and this new news. I knew without asking that my sister had called Nick too, telling him the news first so I didn't have to but also so he would know to watch out for me. I'm not sure what they were worried I was going to do, or where I was going to go. I was a hundred years pregnant and couldn't go more than fifteen minutes without having to use a bathroom, making it a rather inconvenient time for an impulse road trip.

Plus, I was breathing. Nick pulled me into his chest, hard, and my bags fell out of my hands and spilled out onto the porch as I felt myself stiffen like I was encased in protective shellac. When he released me, I sunk onto the porch steps and pulled up my skirt, letting the sun hit my legs. "Porch needs painting," I said, scraping at the flaking boards with my fingernail. I looked at him. It was hard to even remember what he had looked like back when we met, when I was sixteen and he was eighteen with hair down his back and the teen angst to match. Now he was a clean-cut school teacher and the father of our three–almost four–babies, a complete and total transformation that had happened so slowly that I often forgot it had ever been anything but this way. I wanted to tell him about the woman at my window and how amazing it was to be able to exhale, but it felt private, and anyways, I wasn't sure he could possibly understand. His mother was still very much alive and also incredible, and while Nick and I had each been terrible in our ways to our mothers when we were younger, only mine had ever been terrible back to me.

The rich smell of the beef stew I'd left in the Crock-Pot that morning wafted out onto the porch through the open door, and I gagged, trying to remember what it had felt like to chop garlic and onions and plan a dinner like an idiot, like everything wasn't going to be changed in an instant with four little words from my sister: "It's Mom. She's gone." I pulled myself up and padded barefoot into the kitchen, dumped the Crock-Pot contents into the garbage disposal and watched it swirl into the drain until all evidence of it was gone, and then Nick and I told the kids that their grandmother was gone.

We stayed out on the porch in the showoff-y splendor of the September sunshine for a long time that night. For a lot of it, Maria, then eight and the spitting image of my sister when she was young, stayed next to me. Together we watched Gabby, then three, dance in front of us, twirling circles in the lawn.

"Mommy," Maria asked eventually, leaning into me enough that her loose curls brushed into my lap, "is it okay for Gabby to keep dancing even if Nona is dead now?"

The question stayed with me for a long time, through the aftermath of that evening as we tried to maintain our routine, attending to dinner (pizza to replace the beef stew) and doing the dishes and giving baths and tucking children into their beds, but long after that too. It's not that I struggled to answer her. On the contrary. The quick assurance that yes, it was absolutely okay to keep dancing, necessary even, spilled out of my mouth with such force that one of *her* curls lifted in the breeze of my breath. It's not that at all. It's this: I wish so hard that I had just grabbed Maria's hand and pulled her down from the peeling porch and onto the grassy dance floor. I wish that I had danced that evening too, even if it took me a while to find my rhythm. Even if what came out looked more like a convulsion at first than a celebration. Even if I had to dance, weeping and wailing, on my knees.

Or even more than that, it's that I wish I hadn't waited until I'd been clubbed over the head with senseless tragedy to realize that I should have been dancing all along. I'd wasted so much of my life looking around at the great pain in the world and the great pain in my heart and thought: With all this misery in the world, why would anyone dance, ever? You'd have to be ignorant, I would have said, or even insensitive, to dance in the face of such things.

And then in one delayed exhale, I'd seen I'd had it wrong all along. The lesson isn't that we should dance in spite of the suffering. It's that we should dance ourselves right through the suffering. We have to court that shit, get up close to it, extend a hand and make a dance partner out of it, twirling it around in the front lawn until we are both so dizzy that we can't tell anymore where the suffering ends and where the joy begins. Because what naturally follows, to anyone finally paying attention to the fact that each breath is a miracle, is the realization that the next one isn't guaranteed. And we can be grateful for the one we're in or we can panic about the one that we hope is next to come, but we can't do both, not really, not well.

So now I almost always try to put my focus on the former. And sometimes that's easy. Sometimes I look at the faces of my children or my husband or my coffee or my house after the cleaners have come, and life feels for a sweet second so much like the full-on miracle it is that it swells up in a huge rush, a gratitude-tsunami that threatens to pick me up and carry me along in its wake for miles, eventually depositing me into a tide pool where I can float, delirious and drunk off my own thanks.

Other times it's harder to find the miraculousness of it all, and I have to really try, reaching and rooting around for it the way I do for the blankets when I wake up cold in the middle of the night and realize I've kicked everything down to the foot of the bed in my sleep; it's dark and my limbs are drugged heavy with sleep and every movement made towards trying to wrap back up in the familiar softness is a challenge.

And yeah, more often it's the latter, like if I have a big pimple, or all four of my children are all wailing holy hell together in chorus, or my insomnia comes back, or someone cuts me off in traffic, or I wake to a small child yelling frantic from the kitchen, "Holy guacamole, I didn't even know yogurt could do that!" and I know before I even open my eyes that there will be an unspeakable mess awaiting. There are days even now where I will be hit with a sense of loss so strong that it knees me, knocking me down and out with a longing for my mother so deep that I have to fight my way back up to standing. The truth still is, and probably always will be, that sometimes it gets cold and dark in my life, either because for some God-knows-why reason we live where it's winter for six months out of the year, or because my depression comes back every once in a while and I forget to be easily awestruck by this breath still moving in and out.

But I do try to always come back to that moment in the car when the air left my lungs, to blink, to rearrange, to remember the importance of the foggy circle of breath on the car window, or the curve of Maria's curl against my wrist, or the way Gabby lifted her face up to the light while she spun in the yard. And when it's winter and it's dark and it's cold, a blanket of snow can be a very glittery reminder of all of the blessings we can't help but take for granted most days: a warm place to live, a soft space to sit, the unbelievable gift of heat in the vents and yellow lights that glow from the windows when you pull in the driveway after your day because yes, some days are dark, but just because it's harder to see things in the dark doesn't mean they're not there. It just means I have to work for it a little, breathe deeper and look around, and let things in and let things out, and write words, and go deep and tell the truth and remember, again, what I already know.

I remember too how my mother used to say to me when I was struggling that sometimes the old adage of taking life one day at a time is too much, and it needs to be broken down into something smaller and slightly more manageable like one hour at a time or one minute at a time. And what I know now is that if we really open our eyes and our hearts and look around at all that life has to offer us as a dance partner, we would know the only true way to make it through is to dance, one glorious breath at a time.

6

⎯◇⎯

Sometimes You Just Want to Come Home

The hard truth–the one I still struggle with to this day–is that I'd mostly shut my mother out of my life in those last years before she died. And while it's hard not to wonder what would have happened or could have happened had I been there more, I also know that I did what I had to do in order to survive. Something in me simply closed up. I think that's how it works, how it *has* to work: after a while, the part of us that tries to save someone needs to turn itself off because if it stays on all of the time, we would die from the exposure. There's little but heart-break after heartbreak to be found in chasing after someone who is on their way down into the bottom, and my heart had broken so many times when it came to my mother that eventually I worried it wouldn't work right anymore, that I'd lost my ability to love her at all, that it was just an ugly mass of scar tissue held together with duct tape and spite.

I think part of it is instinct, too, basic biology: when something has hurt us, our bodies want to run, to pull our hand back quick from the hot burn of the stove and never touch it again, and in the moment, I think that's life saving, I really do. When your hand is on fire and the pain is all-consuming, you can't stand there and think, "But I've made so many wonderful dinners on this stove"; all you can think is, "Get me away from this right now." My mother had hurt me, and eventually I'd given in and let myself run. I had to, but I'd also be lying if I told you that was the easy option. None of this mess was ever easy.

A therapist I saw for a while back then told me it was harder in many ways to grieve a person who was still living than it was to grieve one who had actually died. I didn't know about all that, not yet, but I knew that I felt like an orphan even when my mother was living less than a mile away and I could easily run into her at the grocery store. I couldn't talk about her, not even to my kids, because I was never able to keep my emotions from dancing across my face or my eyes from clouding at her name. I didn't want them to know about the pain; it was my pain, and they didn't need it in their lives. I didn't want to tell Jack that the first time I ever saw my mother drunk in my life was on a Tuesday morning when she was supposed to be baby-sitting him, how I'd walked into her house and seen her standing there, disheveled and disoriented in a bathrobe that wasn't closed all the way, and it was like walking into a space you've lived in all of your life but the furniture has been rearranged and you just can't seem to get your bearings. I think that was probably the last time I ever took for granted that I could just go home when I needed to, when I needed help or things got hard or I needed my mother. And part of that is embarrassing, really, this silly idea I had that I could grow up and leave the house and make a life and yet things where I came from would always be the way I left them; that I'd always be able to come home, no matter what.

I didn't cut her out then, though, not that first time. I'd thought that first time was a fluke, a very human overindulgence or medication mix-up or, I don't know, early morning vodka and orange juice celebration. Whatever it was it seemed innocent enough and forgettable, until it kept happening. Until one afternoon we found her, drunk and unresponsive, lying on her bedroom floor in just her underwear. My sister had gotten there first that day, called 911, and then called me. "It's Mom," she said, and I raced there, not even conscious of the drive, not sure what I had to offer anyone in terms of help or salvation but sure that I had better get it to them as soon as I could. Except when I saw my mother there, unconscious and almost naked and so thin that I could count her ribs from across the room, I was unable to do anything but the most useless thing of all: burst into tears.

I'm still not proud of it, the way I just stood there frozen and crying while my little sister took care of business around me. It was that same sensation again, the way I was standing in the house I grew up in, the same bedroom I had retreated to a million times in the middle of the night when I was scared or had a nightmare or it thundered, but it just all felt so *unfamiliar*. It could have been tangential, I suppose, since my mother had recently redone everything: painting the turquoise walls white and pulling up the shag carpet to expose the hardwoods underneath. There were new linens on the bed and a tasteful hand-quilted spread I didn't recognize. Together it would have been gorgeous, except it was off somehow, the sheets rumpled and dingy where she had laid in them for the last few days, the new shades pulled tight against the daylight outside. I couldn't get my bearings, couldn't reconcile the scene playing out in front of me—my mother unconscious and flaccid while my sister tried to dress her—with the woman who'd raised me, so severe and polished. There's a sense of unmooring that comes when we realize our parents are human too, that they can break, that maybe they are breaking right there in front of us on their bedroom floor. I need to go home, something inside me called out, and yet I found I didn't know what that meant anymore. I'd always thought of this place as my home, the house I grew up in, sure, but also the woman who had raised me. But now I had my own house, my own babies, my own beginnings of roots that were trying desperately to sink down into an earth. I think in a lot of ways I'd been hesitant to swap one for the other, afraid to turn my back on my mother as she fell, never realizing then that home is not a static place we reside in as much as it is an ever-evolving space we come into—and out of—as we need to.

In her last few years of life, my mother had started going to church again. My family didn't go to church when I was growing up, didn't talk of God, didn't say grace around the table or get on our knees bedside in the evenings. You don't know to miss a thing you've never had, either, so it wasn't until later when my friends were throwing first communion parties that I thought to ask my mother why not. Because she'd had enough of all that growing up, she'd answered, her voice pinched like she had tasted something bitter. So it surprised me when she quietly started up again. "You're doing what?" I said when she asked me if I wanted to come along one Sunday. "Are you serious?"

Eventually curiosity won out and I did go along. It was confusing to me, all the sitting and standing and kneeling, but even more confusing was how hard I had to work to keep from bursting into tears every time the music swelled. It wasn't the mass itself that really moved me, although it was beautiful in its own right. It was more the way my mother seemed so small and docile there next to me, her softness a stark contrast to the hardness of both the wooden pew we sat in and her normal personality. She'd made a life out of being sharp enough to draw blood if you bumped up against her, left her family as soon as she could, rebuilt herself after a hundred divorces, risen to the top of her career. As a rule, when we were growing up, she did not ask for help, not ever, not even when she probably should have. She taught me early on that if we relied on no one and asked for nothing, we could protect ourselves from disappointment. Church Mom was different, though, delicate somehow. I watched her walk back towards me after receiving communion, her hands still clasped together and her head bowed contrite, and I wondered what she prayed for, this woman who would rather have died than admit she needed help. Did she ask God for the things she wouldn't ask anyone else for?

I asked her over a post-church dinner how she could want to be at church again after hating it all those years. "Didn't the church hurt you?" I asked, remembering the stories she told of Catholic school nuns that hit and shamed, or the disappointed way the church saw her many divorces, or women's reproductive rights, or gay marriage.

She nodded.

"So why go back now, after all this time?"

She sighed. "Sometimes you just want to be able to go home," she said, and I didn't get it but I wanted to act like I did because it sounded so grown-up. So I didn't ask her any follow-up questions, like how could someone want to go back to something that maybe wasn't great or even good, or how could the church be her home if *we* were supposed to be her home, my sister and me and the life we'd all built together, and that house where a couple of years later we'd find her unconscious and worry for a second she was dead before we realized that nope, she was just drunk, because home can be found in a lot of places sometimes all at once, and one of those, for some of us, is at the bottom of a top-shelf bottle of Russian vodka.

When my mother called one evening and asked me if I would consider joining the church, I surprised myself by saying yes.

"Really?" my mother asked, after a pause. I think I surprised her too. "You will?"

I was sitting outside on the front stoop smoking a cigarette while I talked to her, a holdover from yet another bad habit I'd had as a teenager that I still allowed myself to indulge in from time to time. It would prove to be the last cigarette I'd have in a very long time, though, because while I didn't know it then, I was newly pregnant with Maria. I took a long drag and exhaled the smoke into the night. The air was still mild but smelled subtly like fall, and I could feel the sense of seasons turning. Eight years later, my sister would call to tell me my mother was gone, and immediately I would feel again that same sense of time shifting.

"Sure," I said. "Let's do it."

We went to classes together for months, my mother picking me up every Saturday morning to drive me to church until I realized she was arriving a little more intoxicated each week and I offered to drive instead. We would sit in those same pews, me trying to swallow back my morning sickness and her trying to stay awake. Often she would lose the battle and her head would drop onto my shoulder while she softly snored, my eyes daring the other women in the class or the steely nun who led it to go ahead, say something. They never did.

By the time Easter weekend arrived, I was five months pregnant and my mother was clearly an alcoholic. She didn't show for the rehearsal, which is where I learned I was going to be dunked in a pool of holy water. "Wait, what?" I said, wondering if I could get an exemption because of the baby. "I have to go all the way under?" When I'd agreed to do it a few months earlier I had imagined a gentle sprinkling of water on my forehead like I'd seen done to babies, enough to give me a dewy glow under the hot lights of the altar but not enough so as to give me the look of a person who'd been saved mid-drown.

"You can freshen up afterwards in the back," the steely nun said, as if that settled it.

I called my mother twice that afternoon to make sure she was awake and coming. "Leave me alone," she said. "I'm getting ready."

"Well don't make yourself too pretty," I said. "Some of us will be all wet."

She laughed.

"I'm doing this for you, you know," I said, half under my breath.

"You better bring a hair dryer with you," was all she said back.

It was pretty though, the ceremony. I hadn't paid as much attention as I should have to the details and I fumbled over what to say when, saying "thanks, you too!" out of habit when the priest said "the body of Christ" and handed me the wafer, for instance. I wasn't sure whether or not it was appropriate to plug my nose in a pool full of holy water and as a result had an ugly choking fit and thought for a second I might pass out. (You know what's even less appropriate? Having to blow holy water out of your nose.) When it was evident I was going to live I ran back to the rectory to dry off, reapplying my makeup next to a recycling bin full of the rectory's empty gallon-sized liquor jugs. "See?" I thought, running my hands through hair warmed from the dryer as fast as I could. "She's not the only one."

Afterwards, over the tea and cookies we nibbled in the harshly lit parish rec hall, my mother told me the acoustics of the cathedral allowed for the sound of my hair dryer to be amplified so loud it drowned out the bishop.

We laughed.

"I did this for you, you know," we both said to each other, as if on cue, and looking back I think we were both telling the truth.

I'd thought for a while that we would make it into a thing, us and the church, going together weekly with whatever combination of my own little family I could finagle into the process. But if what I'd witnessed those few months together in my church classes was the beginning of her unraveling, the process had picked up steam shortly thereafter. Soon enough I was rooted in my own life of motherhood and chaos and she was rooted in her illness and we barely overlapped at all, unless it was by accident in the frozen food section, and the therapist had been right: it was terribly hard. Grieving a living person, I decided, was like walking around all day long with an open wound that never had any hope of healing because there was no closure, not yet, and especially not while my mother was everywhere I looked.

So eventually, in order to protect myself, I tried to tear it all down and dismantle my past. One by one, I took the pictures of my mother down from my walls. I threw out the greeting cards she'd sent on birthdays, then the Christmas gifts and mementos, and eventually, anything that reminded me of my childhood at all. Like the vodka I'd poured down the sink during our failed intervention attempts, I tried to pour my mother out of my house, thinking in doing so I had a better shot at cleaving her cleanly out of my heart. I remembered how she'd told me the only way to protect yourself from disappointment was to rely on no one, ever, and so I trained myself to stop expecting her to be there at all, which hurt like hell until eventually–in what is either a huge accomplishment or a total abomination, I'm still not sure–the callouses built up enough and I stopped feeling any of it altogether.

And then she died.

I sat in the same pew at my mother's funeral that I'd sat in for my baptism, waiting to feel something–anything–again, convinced that I had insulated myself so much against the pain while my mother was still alive that I would never find my way to honest grief now that she was gone. But of course, even though she was gone, my mother was still everywhere in that church. I remembered the weight of her head on my shoulder as she slept through my church classes, the way her cropped hair tickled my cheek and her breath had gotten slower and softer as she fell deeper into it. I hadn't been to church in years, had never really seriously gone on my own at all, and then stopped going entirely when she did. I still didn't know the right words or when to sit or stand, but at my mother's funeral mass, I was first in line to receive communion. I turned to walk away, echoing what I'd seen her do with the bow of my head and the way my hands clasped contrite in front of me, but instead of closing my eyes I watched the rows of mourners file past. I'd ignored my mother's life for years, tried to unweave what was hers from what was mine, and yet there in front of me was all the stuff we shared: friends, family, neighbors, community. And it was laid plain what I had not let myself see: that despite every effort I'd made, my mother and I were knit together, our lives and our blood so intertwined that it would have been impossible to separate myself in any real and meaningful way.

One evening a few days later, we were having dinner and Maria tilted her head just so, smiled at something I said, and I was struck with the force of memory. "God, you look just like your grandmother," I said without thinking, realizing it was the first time I had mentioned her name with that kind of ease in years. Other small stirrings of memory started to bubble around inside of me like carbonation, things I had shoved down now occasionally rising to the surface and popping. All at once, I would see us as we, too, had sat around a dinner table laughing, or the way she rested her hand on my back after a nightmare. I remembered her cheering for me while I raced around the track in high school, or shopping together for my senior prom dress. I would hear a song in the car and remember us singing together on our way to summer vacation.

I'd smell her perfume on a crowded elevator and be ten again, climbing into her bed, resting my head in the warm space she'd made on her pillow.

What was happening to me, I wondered, nursing the ache in my heart that was familiar in the way that any muscle will ache when you try to use it for the first time after years of atrophy. I proceeded with caution, opening to her the way I would ease myself into a cold lake: one inch of soft flesh at a time, protective, ready to recoil and run at the slightest provocation. But of course, none came. The worst had already happened, which meant there were no more disappointments to protect myself from.

Emboldened, I disappeared into the attic for hours, searching through a decade of castoffs until I found it: the picture of her in a small frame that I wasn't even sure I had anymore. I carried it downstairs, pointed away from me like a small child carrying scissors, and put it on a shelf in the back corner of a dark room where I was sure to rarely see it. A few days later I moved it more into the light, and again a few days after that, until it sat on the dresser next to my bed and was the first thing I saw in the morning when the sun came through the blinds to wake me up and I would remember, my breath catching in my throat where the lump of contempt no longer sat. There was something else there now in its place. Grief? Maybe. Maybe love. I'd started to see how the two are really just different flavors of the same thing, or maybe two halves of the same whole.

And isn't this a story of homecoming, when you really think about it? Because I remembered how on that day when we'd called 911, years before, I'd stood there and cried like a useless dolt until I heard the sirens and walked into my mother's closet to watch the ambulance arrive in the window, and thank God. Because while both my mother and her bedroom had become unrecognizable to me at that point, the closet was still untouched. There were the same rows of career clothes lining the wall, the familiar pairs of heels stacked up along the corner. The smell of my mother's perfume hung in the air, the same scent she had always worn for as long as I could remember, and I closed my eyes and inhaled deep. It was easy then to remember what it felt like to be small, hiding under these racks of suits and dresses, playing dress-up with the neat rows of heels. My sister tended to our mother, and I fingered the hanging silk scarves, remembering her wrapping my curls up in them when I was little and us taking pictures. In the back corner there was the dress she wore to my wedding, still in the dry cleaner's bag. I could see her at the reception, showing off her ballroom dancing lessons and leaning in close as she passed me, reminding me not to drink too much, and me laughing as I gently pushed her away, like we were just your normal everyday mother and daughter, dancing in circles next to each other. Like it was going to stay that way forever.

So maybe I had it wrong when I assumed my mother should always be my mother and my home should always be my home and nothing was going to change, ever, but maybe the idea that it was all lost forever was wrong too. Because, like that small space I'd found in the closet that had stood the test of time, I had pieces in my memory that were unmarred by the losses of time. And now, finally safe, I willed myself to remember all the stuff I'd held down. I stared at myself for hours in my bathroom mirror. Did I have her eyes? Her smile? Her hands? I remembered her laugh, how it used to tumble forth at the most inopportune moments and everyone else couldn't help but laugh too, even when they were the punch line. I cooked her dinner recipes and put on her diamonds and smelled the remnants of her perfume—the smell from her closet and my entire childhood—on the clothes she had handed down to me years before and eventually, I released the sea of tears I had held buried inside for ten years.

Today, I don't remember her at all like she was those last years. Time and grief have softened those sharp edges into something different, and I like to remember her now the way she looks in that picture that sits next to my bed: her head tilted up towards the camera or the sun or the person taking the picture, which probably was my father but I'm not sure. It doesn't make sense that I could remember her like that because she was young when it was taken, probably hadn't even had me yet, but it feels right. And if I squint my eyes just right and let the sepia-toned edges blur, the circle completes, and she is me. A little more, and she is Maria. Like the picture itself, it took her dying for me to find her again, but I have, and what I found is that she is in me, always was, always will be. Faith is still a complicated road for me, but on my best days I know in my heart that in dying she really did go home, and it was there where I was able to find her again.

7

---◊---

The Gift of Sisterhood

When I was growing up, my mother always made me write thank-you notes for anything I ever received. And (this will not shock you) I was usually kind of an asshole about it. Eventually she got fed up with my protests and just wrote me a script: "Thank you for the gift of X. I will use it to X." "Just fill in the X's based on the gift," she said. "Just freaking do it." And so I did, begrudgingly, usually creating passive-aggressive masterpieces that looked like this:

Dear Auntie,
Thank you for the gift of money. I will use it to spend.
Love, Liz

I thought of those tortured thank-you notes when I struggled, again, to express how grateful I was for the gifts I had been given in the weeks following my mother's death. I sat down with a pen and some pretty cardstock and wondered, what is the best way to say thank you for holding me up? For reminding me how to breathe? How do you properly express gratitude for not just the food that was dropped off and the cupcakes that were baked but the endless conversations that were held where I simply talked in rambling circles and my friends did their best to follow, my mind unable to grasp the reality of what was happening around me? How did I truly thank my best friend for dropping her new life in Maine, seven hours away, and driving to me the second she heard I needed her? Or for the way the neighborhood women had—unbeknownst to me—come into my house while my family was at my mother's funeral and cleaned it and filled it with light and food and coffee and drinks and all of the people we loved, so when we arrived, it was the first in a very long time where I truly felt like I had come home?

It seems silly to admit this now, but for a long time, women straight up scared me. When I was still pretty young (and as my own relationship with my mother got more and more difficult to navigate), something inside me decided it would be simpler to just avoid having girlfriends as much as possible, a decision that proved relatively easy to follow through on because the truth was, girlfriends were not exactly knocking down my door. I'm actually still pretty terrible at letting people all the way in, which is funny because I have a blog where I tell intimate stories about my life, but hey, life is funny like that. When it comes to making friends, I've taken a long roundabout route filled with plenty of small annoying potholes, like that time I tried to be friendly to someone who I forgot hated me from high school, but also some real and true heartbreak. As it is with anything important and worth it, the risk of getting ourselves hurt is real, and none of it is easy.

Many years ago, I used to work with a woman who hated me, believe it or not. And I mean *hated me* hated me. There's an expression in the online world, "Bitch Eating Crackers," or "BEC" for short because life is much too busy to be insulting people in full actual words. Anyway, what it means is that you dislike a person so much that they could be minding their own business and doing something totally inane, like eating crackers, and still it irritates the crap out of you. You're all, "Look at her over there, eating those crackers like that. Ugh. What a bitch."

So yeah, I was this coworker's BEC. Now, the reality is I am probably a whole lot of people's BEC, which is understandable because I write stories on the internet and sometimes mention my lady parts, and this pisses off a surprisingly large amount of people. Also I am an over-sharing hermit, an oxymoron which is confusing even to me. One second I'm all, "I love you! Let's be soulmates forever and never be apart!" and the next I'm MIA, on a kitchen counter wiping/Netflix bender for two weeks where my family only survives on what groceries I can order in because the idea of leaving the house to go the store feels oppressively exhausting. It doesn't help that I basically came out of the womb with my resting bitch face already on point and that I'm hopelessly socially awkward. Take, for example, this interaction I had recently with a group of lovely women I had never met but live near, so I was trying extra hard not to say anything truly stupid in front of:

Lovely Lady 1, talking to Lovely Lady 2: "Yeah, so I was out walking Herman . . ."

Me (who was not even being spoken to): "Aw, is Herman your dog?"

Lovely Lady 1: "Um, hi. Yes."

Me: "Cool. That's my hemorrhoid's name."

This is the kind of thing that happens again and again when I try to talk to other people, so usually I would totally understand why I am a good BEC candidate, but with this particular coworker it stung because we had once been on our way to becoming actual friends. Aided by the proximity that working together brings, we had made it a few steps successfully past my resting bitch face and my awkward small talk about body parts and into that territory where you have started to bare little tiny pieces of your soul like appetizers, served up to gauge the other person's reaction so you can decide when and if they will be ready for the main course of your particular flavor of crazy.

And man, if it hadn't been nice to have a friend. We worked in a restaurant together, a busy, ridiculous, low-priced family-friendly shit show of a place that wasn't going to win any culinary awards, and I've always said it was the hardest I've ever worked in my life, those double shifts on my feet running big trays of food and trying to smile as people let their kids throw their spaghetti on my shoes. I've done more important things since then, maybe, but nothing as physical and usually not as hungover as I was then. So it was nice to have someone next to me as we slogged through it, Sisyphus pushing the bread-crumb-heavy meatball up the mountain, sure, but at least we were doing it together.

And then one day she just hated me. Always quick on the uptake, it took me a while to realize the tides had turned. I followed her around the restaurant for a few more days until eventually she turned around in frustration and maybe a little malice and made it plain: she did not like me, not one bit.

I was devastated. All of the sudden I knew with instant clarity that she was probably my favorite friend ever, and I wondered how I would ever be able to get married to the fiancé I didn't yet have in the wedding that was not scheduled if she wasn't my maid of honor.

How would I have the kids that wouldn't appear for years and years if she couldn't be their godmother?

How would I someday watch that iconic episode of *Grey's Anatomy* where Christina names Meredith her person if I didn't have this exact woman (who couldn't stand me) as my person?

Did I mention I can't remember her last name? Or what she looked like? Or if her first name started with a *J* or a *G*? Did I mention how she was kind of mean even when we were friends and I was always a little unsure if I could trust her, and how some part of me was always concerned that maybe I should have run away as fast as I could in the opposite direction before she stabbed me?

But none of that matters when we get rejected. None of that matters when someone you think is on your team reveals themselves to be rooting against you. None of that matters when you put yourself out there only to have someone say, "Yeah, no thanks actually, I'm all set" as they back away slowly and carefully, hands raised as if to say, "Not only do I not enjoy your particular flavor of crazy, Liz, but I'm a little afraid it might be contagious."

None of it mattered, no, but none of it invalidated either what I had seen in my heart when she and I had started to open up to each other, which was this: life is hard and we need each other. I mean, maybe not specifically her and me, we probably didn't need each other, at least not anymore. And my natural reaction for a long time after that particular wound was to close up and nurse my ego and say, "See? This is why I've avoided women friends for so long, you guys." Except I went on to do some big stuff, clean up my life and get married and have babies and start a career and eventually, lose my mother to a swirling tempest of struggle, and I can unequivocally tell you: there is no surviving that shit alone. Nope. None of it. Don't try. Despite the risks of continuing to put ourselves out there, despite the potential heartbreak when we don't fit together exactly perfectly, we need each other.

We need the older, more experienced women in our lives who have walked before and remember, the ones who can leave us a trail of wisdom crumbs behind for us to follow when we are lost in the dark.

We need the ones who walk with us at our side, whispering those two sweetest words like a salve to our tired soul: Me too.

And we need the ones who walk behind, not there yet, who look at us with big eyes and remind us of where we have been and how we have grown and what we have conquered and how much we still have yet to learn.

We need other women who know what it feels like to split into a thousand pieces as they give small pieces of themselves to their family, their job, their friends, and their neighbors, women who see our suffering and resist the natural impulse to shrink away, who meet it instead with an ear, a shoulder, an embrace, a meal. Women to teach us to stop apologizing for what we are not sorry for and to love ourselves enough to say no. Women who have taken their bodies back and learned to love the soft places. Women whose scars and stretch marks map a story of survival and strength for them to consult whenever they are feeling lost. And we need the women who create: babies or art or sustenance or beauty or words, worship, a testament of our feminine belief that yes, still, even now, the world is worth making better. Women who carry themselves and their babies through a world that still sometimes scares them with heads held high and shoulders back because they are the truest kind of warriors: those who are afraid and do it anyway.

And for me personally? Well, I need women who I can regularly text things to like "is it normal to . . . (eat an entire bag of potato chips in one sitting or spend the day in bed wallowing in self-loathing or scream at my children so loudly that my throat hurts or burst into tears at a dog food commercial)?" And they'll say "yes" or "of course" or "I'm doing that very same thing right now!" even if they aren't, because truth is less important, technically, than sisterhood.

Let's be clear: I love my husband a lot. He's my soul mate and he's also the one who lets me stay in bed on Sunday mornings while he makes eggs and toast for the family and I pretend to sleep while really scrolling Facebook uninterrupted on my phone under the covers and *it's heaven,* but there are things he doesn't get. I can't turn to him in the grocery store when someone walks by with one of those babies that is so new that the pinkness hasn't worn off yet and they are still curled up in belly-shape and say, "Honey, my uterus aches just looking at that," without him turning grey and running away, fearful that I might actually try to talk him into having a fifth. I can't explain to him in any logical way how my whole body aches for my mother still, and not just on the regular days like Mother's Day and her birthday but on Wednesdays when it rains, because there is no logic to it, and he's not a daughter, and my mom and I hardly even got along when she was alive anyway. I love my husband and my children and they are my everything, but they can't be my only thing; there's no surviving like that. I still need women, we all do, even if that means we assume the risk that comes with putting our whole selves out there.

I remembered the BEC incident many years later when my oldest daughter, eleven now, was waiting for me when I walked in the door from work. Before I had set my bag down, she was sobbing at me, her face crumpled under the stress of crying out whatever she had been holding in.

"What's wrong?" I asked.

"So-and-so's having a party," she started, naming one of her friends and pausing to wipe her nose on her sleeve. "I'm not invited."

And just like that, all of the years' worth of wisdom that had come in between me and my BEC coworker flew out of me in one long exhale. Because right then, I was back there, watching a girl decide I was her BEC and move on, unbeknownst to me, from a friendship I was still very much invested in. I could still feel the betrayal hot in my gut as if it had just happened, the way the tears burned at my eyes, that sinking affirmation of the fear that runs through so many of our heads, saying we're not good enough, no one will understand, and most importantly, we don't belong.

And I stood there in my foyer in my coat and my heels and tried my best to summon words to make everything better for the little love of my life who stood before me as broken-hearted as I'd been. "People are terrible" seemed harsh. "Never trust anyone" was the wrong answer. I had nothing, I realized. Except that wasn't exactly true either. What I had was my compassion.

So I stepped out of my heels and the shadow of my past. I shed my coat and the weight of the grudges I might have still been carrying against my old coworker and a bunch of other past digressions and slights and hurts and betrayals, including that one chick from high school who still has zero interest in being my friend, for those of you keeping track. They weren't terribly bad grudges, either. I wasn't going to boil someone's bunny or send them a horse's head, but maybe if I saw one of them in the grocery store and their hands were full and they needed to reach the good ice cream on the top shelf of the freezer, I would probably reach in and grab it and then run away cackling with it tucked under my arm. But either way, they were grudges that had been carried around with me for much too long, I finally saw. And deciding to let go of them then and there was so freeing that all of a sudden there was all sorts of space in my heart to wrap my little girl up inside of.

And I got down to where I could be eye level with her. I wrapped her in my arms and rocked slow and said the two words I did know to be true: "I know. I know, I know, I know, I know." Because didn't I? Don't you? Doesn't everyone know what that feels like, some personal version of the BEC birthday noninvitation heard 'round the world? Who would ever wish such pain on their kid? For that matter, who would ever risk leaving the house again, making that awkward small talk, trying to peel past the layers of defensiveness and shellac until we get to the tender meat on the inside, the parts of us who still long so badly to be heard, to be seen, to be understood?

And that I did know the answer to. It's me. I would. Not every day and maybe occasionally not for weeks at a time but eventually, yes, I would take the risk again. The truth is I'll risk my BEC and her betrayal a thousand times over because the other side, the people who don't walk away, the people who *do* invite you to their parties, they're more than worth it. Human connection is always worth it, because human connection is what Maria and I had there in that moment, no longer mother and daughter for a moment but members of this community, this sisterhood of people who had shared an experience and understood. That's what matters, more than anything else.

So this is what I told my daughter, eventually, once the sting of her wound had settled into a dull ache in the background and we had words again. I told her how we have to keep taking this risk, over and over and over again every time we leave the house, my shy daughter and her shy mama and everyone else of us who has ever felt insecure or weird or a little like maybe there couldn't possibly be another person on the planet who would completely get who we are. Because there are people out there for us, our people, I promise. They're not everyone and they may not even be most of us, but they're there. There are people who are made up of the same things as you are, people who have visited the same places and walked the same path and climbed out of the same trenches. This is what is holy and divine to me about female friendships in a world where they are vastly undervalued and frankly, a little scary. Because what is far scarier than that is being Sisyphus all alone, thanklessly pushing your own pile of shit up the hill with no women to be the mirror that we bounce ourselves off of, the way we know we're not alone.

In my yoga training there was a phrase that was thrown around a lot: holding space. It's a lovely phrase, poetic even, and I was immediately drawn to it. "Holding space for somebody" sounded so intimate and yet selfless, and I knew instantly that I wanted to do it and more importantly, have it done for me. Except I had no idea what it actually meant. How the hell do you hold space for somebody? What is that, even? It sounds big and heavy, the kind of thing only healthy and put-together people can do well, and certainly not people who cry at dog food commercials. I can't even hold myself together, much less hold another person's space together for them.

Except I think that's what this is, this sisterhood. I think it's holding space. I think those texts I get that say, "Yes, Liz, it's perfectly okay to call in sick to work because you have a large pimple on the side of your forehead," or the side-hugs that I'm given when I miss my mother because I smelled her perfume in the elevator or saw her eyes in Luca's or for no reason at all, are exactly that. These are my people, the kind who tell me it's reasonable to have feelings for loungewear that Nicholas Sparks could write a novel about, even when we all know it's not reasonable at all. And on the days when I really do fail, making the kinds of mistakes that no one is optimistic enough to pretend aren't at least a little mistake-y, they say, "It's okay, Liz. Just try harder tomorrow," and it's like a little space to breathe, right there just for me.

That's what was given to me, really, in those weeks after my mother's death. No one was going to be able to take away the pain or the anger or the confusion, we all knew that. But what they could do is hold space for the enormity of what I felt, and what that meant was I didn't have to hold it all myself. It's like how many hands make light work; many hearts make light too, and that was exactly the thing I needed there in the dark. There's only one way to say thank you for that, I believe, and that is to do it for as many people as I can as often as I can. And also this:

Dear Friend,

Thank you for the gift of sisterhood. I will use it to survive.

Love, Liz

8

---◊---

A Letter to My Mother about My Daughter

She's been holding my hand again, Mom. Maria has. And not just because I make her, the way I used to stand still in the parking lot and not let her take any steps until she had safely placed her little kid hand inside mine. No, this is different; it's borne of her need, and it's raw and unpredictable. I don't know if it's because she was rocked by your death or maybe it's because she saw *me* rocked by it, and maybe both of those things have bled into each other because we are connected, the same way you and I used to be, before. We watch TV together now, sharing a couch and maybe even a blanket, and her hand will reach out suddenly when I'm not paying attention and grip me with a fierceness that never fails to surprise me. Or when

I tuck her in at night, kiss her forehead, and say I love you (because ever since you died I always say I love you), and she touches my hand when she says, "I love you too, Mom," back to me with a squeeze.

I love you too, Mom. I do hope you know that.

The other day even, walking her into school—the place where public displays of parental affection go to die—she held my hand the whole way in. That one made me a little fluttery, like I was being given a gift. I took it. I needed it.

She's amazing, Mom, this girl. Remember how she used to go into herself when she was little and tired or overstimulated or just done? How she would hunch her shoulders and bow her wispy-haired head and dim the light in her eyes and you just knew she'd left? I think you called it "turtling," if I remember correctly. Well, now she's bigger and almost as tall as me and plays on the boy's baseball team with her shoulders thrown back and her head held high and what looks like yards of golden curls tucked up under her hat. She takes my breath away, and I want to tell you everything about her except I know you already know, you must. Where else would she get this strength from?

So instead I will tell you this.

I have your ring now, the one from Dad, and I wear it on my right hand. She was holding that hand the other night and if I looked at our hands together and squinted just enough to blur the edges, it was us, you and me. And I saw it, the future of us, of you and me but also of her and me, the inevitability of the hand-holding leading into not-hand-holding and the separation that we all know is to come.

There's so much advice out there on raising girls, advice both solicited and unsolicited thrown in heaps around my feet, but no one yet has been able to tell me how to stop seeing your face in hers. No one has told me how to stay open to the love of women in my life after losing the most important one. More important, no one has told me how to stay friends with a girl who I know is going to break my heart someday just by virtue of growing up.

Because I want to turtle too, or at least I did, after you died. It was hard watching them grow so fast before, but now there is the pulsing reminder of you—of how it could all change, of how all things eventually end—pounding like a heartbeat through everything that happens.

She will be a teenager soon enough, and a woman after that, and maybe a mother or a wife too. I think she'll be a leader; she's fearless like that, and the world will be better for having been touched by her just as I am. But my hand will ache when she sets it down, I know that too. I can already feel the warning of it if I think about it too long, so I don't. I fight the desire to turtle into myself and hide from what I know is going to hurt. I'm going to leave my hand there, awkward and outstretched, fingers parted slightly in gentle waiting, and hope in the depths of my soul that she will take it.

And when the day comes that she doesn't, because it will, if I fall over on the sidewalk in a heartbroken heap in front of the entrance to her school, what I am asking of you is this, Mom: please take my hand and lift me up. Quickly too, and before she sees me lying there. I need her to see me as strong. Just like I used to see you.

9

---◊---

In Between the Black
and White

It never fails.

Every time I write something about motherhood or marriage or life in general being difficult, every time I have the nerve to come out and say something about it being hard some days, or how there is so much pressure to be perfect and happy and selfless and how that is crap because we are still—last I checked—selves that require care and rest and nurturing too, inevitably someone comes at me with their hair on fire throwing around words like *whiny* and *selfish* and *ungrateful*.

And I don't mind so much, not now, not anymore. Since I started writing I've been called every name in the book by angry strangers and occasionally even by people who I know in real life, simply because they thought I was complaining about something that should always be seen as a gift. As if it isn't possible to love our children and our families while being real about sleep deprivation, postpartum depression, and the never-ending mountains of laundry. As if humans are so evolved that we can walk on two feet and attain higher consciousness and travel in space but we can't feel more than one emotion at a time. As if everything in life is always that black and white, all good or all bad, a precious gift or a curse, and the second someone gives voice to the hard stuff it means they have wholly forsaken the entirety of the good.

It's that lie of an idea and the message it sends and the hate it emboldens that I do mind, very much. Because, again, as if. As if every single complicated life out there isn't made up of moments of pain and moments of unbridled joy and moments too of boring minutiae and mundane routine that can be comforting in their repetitiveness or make you feel a little like you're drowning, depending on the day. As if we're not all out there together alternating between struggling and rejoicing from day to day or moment to moment or breath to breath. As if I don't know a single person who hasn't suffered, just like I don't know a single person who hasn't loved or danced or celebrated something, at least once, ever.

One of the things people most remember about my mother was her laugh. It seemed to start deep in her belly and then bubble up and overflow out of her mouth, a loud and sometimes alarming guffaw that she could still pass off as ladylike because she was so gorgeous. It was a thing of legends, incredible and contagious and mentioned over and over in the first weeks after she took her life. "That laugh though," people would say to me, and I would smile, nod. Yup. I know. You would think it would be weird—sacrilege, even—to remember someone who died of depression for their laugh, but I'm finding grief, like everything else in life, isn't as black and white as all that.

Like how my mother died when I was thirty-seven weeks pregnant, and three weeks later I gave birth on my bathroom floor to her last grandson, a baby boy with her blue eyes that she would never meet. I lived for a while then in the space between the two biggest extremes I can think of, birth and death, and the way I would cycle between them so many times in a day made me dizzy. I knew in my bones that it was a miracle, this birth, a gift that was the glue that held my family together through our tragedy, and yet still, I watched myself become obsessed with death too. It's like my mother died and all at once it hit me—my own mortality and the mortality of everyone around me, my husband, my kids, my family and friends and everyone I cared about and even those I didn't. I'm sure I knew that death was inevitable before, on some basic level like we all do, but I didn't think about it all the time like I did now. I had a newborn, the symbol of all that is fresh and new and pure, and yet I felt surrounded by death. Trying to pick a lane between the two was impossible, paralyzing, and occasionally embarrassing. Now I would sit in a restaurant, my husband trying to have a conversation with me, and all I could say were things like, "How much longer do you think the older couple at the table next to us has left to live?" and "How could they be just sitting there, eating fried clams, when they know they're going to die?"

And then one day I remembered how I'd taken prenatal yoga classes and while we laid with our eyes closed in Savasana at the end of the class the teacher would weave her way among us, her soft voice reminding us—us with our finely detailed birth plans and our heavy hopes and expectations—that birth was often full of surprises. Try to make space in your hearts for more than one thing, she'd say. We are complicated and brilliantly made beings, capable of growing life inside of us. Of course we are also capable of feeling more than one thing at a time. We don't have to choose.

When she said to make space in our hearts for surprises, I don't think she meant this particular situation, probably not in the literal sense anyway. She was an amazing teacher (and still is), but I don't think having students whose mother killed herself a couple weeks before they delivered their baby was on her radar, at least not yet. I think she meant that most things in life—especially the big things—usually don't fit neatly into one category, or that nothing really worth it is ever going to be all black or all white. But the sentiment is really the same when you think about it, and think about it I did, often. I thought about how it was okay, had to be, to be frustrated and exhausted and hormonal and in pain while still being overwhelmingly awe-struck and grateful at the gift of new life being brought forth from my body. I thought about how I loved my baby so much and yet sometimes I wanted nothing more than to be able to leave the house without him and catch my breath. I thought about how I already missed my mother fiercely and terribly and yet I wasn't really done being angry at her yet either. And I thought about how the only way I was going to survive the trials of caring for a newborn and healing my postpartum body all while trying to make sense of a loss that had rocked my very core was if I made some space in my broken heart for all of this to exist at the same time.

I'm pretty sure this saved my life, or maybe I'm being dramatic again; it's hard to know now. What I do know is it changed my life, because it allowed me to see how this is always the answer, all of the time. The only way we make it through any of this journey, the good and the bad, the black and the white and everything in between, is to make some space in our hearts for both sides. Because while it's true that my mother had a great laugh, it's also true that she was bitterly unhappy almost all of the time, diagnosed with clinical depression and anxiety disorder, coping with addiction and eventually suicidal. Not many people knew all of this, even at the end, but those of us closest to her can remember her laugh like we just heard it, but also have a hard time recalling when she seemed genuinely happy.

And that scares the crap out of me for a lot of reasons, not the least of which is I have inherited quite a bit from my mother. I have enough of my father in me to mute her beauty, but we have the same exact hands and the same nose and every once in a while that same contagious laugh will spill out of my belly so loud that it scares me. I also share the propensity to melancholy (at my best) and depression (at my worst). By the time I was fifteen, I had already dabbled in more than my fair share of therapy and joined the sizable group of us who warrior on with the help of an antidepressant script. Oh, and I'm a suicide survivor and in recovery from an eating disorder, that too. Thanks to the therapy and the meds and a little of the wisdom that comes with not being fifteen anymore, I'm better at coping now, but crowds still make me anxious and the solitude I long for can still make me lonely, and insomnia has as of yet been my most faithful bed partner. I know the pull of the darkness and I've spent my share of time broken on the bathroom floor, praying that my mother's story is not my own.

So you'd understand why at first I'd tried to arm myself against what I worried was my fate by becoming an expert in my own happiness. These days I know what brings me joy like I know the back of my (mother's) hands. There's the sun shining through the freshly cleaned smudge-free window, the sound of a new bag of potato chips being ripped open, the moment of cracking the binding for the first time on an unread novel. There's the special way a child throws his arms around his mother's neck. There's new sweatpants and old sweatpants and all the sweatpants in between. There are big-bottomed goblets of wine and dark chocolate truffles and all-things bacon and realizing I can still do a cartwheel. There's stepping into an almost-too-hot bath and payday and the smell of garlic and onions sautéing in butter. There are the days the bathroom scale is kind to me and the days my pants look hot on my ass and the moments I pause to catch my breath after a long run and the sweat runs right down my nose and I catch it with my tongue.

I could go on. I'd say this is a good sign, that I could go on, but I don't think it's the thing that's going to save me, either. Because the reality is while lovely, these are simply moments, beautiful but fleeting, and I know that too deep in my soul to be able to rest easy in the comfort of them for very long. And anyway if these moments all strung together into a life are supposed to keep us happy all of the time, it can't help but beg the question that I'm not sure I want to ask: Why weren't our moments enough for my mother?

So I'm not buying it. I mean, sure, these moments string together into a necklace that glitters so prettily in the sun that it's easy sometimes to forget the other side; but it doesn't last. Moments are by nature fleeting, a point that one could argue makes them so lovely in the first place. So no, I don't think we can build a suit of armor against sadness and depression and genetics. Happiness isn't the antidote to depression, nor is it the distraction. Life isn't black and white like that. And if depression is the black and utter joy is the white, then maybe it's in the in-between where the colors are, where we can find sorrow and joy often coexisting right in the same moment. It's where most of us live most of our lives, most of the time. Most of us don't find ourselves in the black and white of either/or very often, nor would we want to. Usually we are both, nuanced, human.

Once I accepted this, I started to see it everywhere, how I am both.

I'm both "I need to get out of here right this second" and "I hope you don't expect me to put that bra back on and go anywhere."

I am at once, "Why do my friends never invite me places anymore?" and "Oh, great, how am I going to get out of this one?"

I am "for the love of all that is holy, if one more person touches me I will fall to the ground in a pile of cold ash" and "someone get over here and snuggle me to sleep, already."

I am "I'm so embarrassed my house is a disaster," and "judge me, FedEx guy, I freaking dare you."

I'm together sucking it all in until the day I die and proud of the beautiful belly I've earned.

I'm both getting up early to do all the things and making love to the snooze button for two hours.

I'm in four-inch heels and big earrings and I'm in bleach-stained sweatpants and fuzzy socks.

I'm quinoa and bone broth and Whole30 and I'm chips and dip and caramel lattes and a too-big glass of chilled wine with ice on the front porch.

I'm the woman who doesn't want vacation to ever end and I'm the one who *cannot wait* to get back home.

I've never been so tired and I've never felt more alive.

I'm the oldest I've ever been and yet I will never again be this young.

I'm a mom, and I'm still me.

I'm afraid, and I'm still doing it.

I'm lonely, and I'm #blessed.

And sometimes my grief hangs heavy from my neck like a stone and drags my gaze down and away from the sun, and other times it shines like light through the hole in my heart, lighting the path.

I'm a mother and yet I'm still her daughter, and she was all of these things too, both sides at once and everything in between. We all are, I'm pretty sure. And every time I sit down and say, "This shit is hard," that's who I am talking to: to me and to my mother and to anyone else who feels like they must be the only one who doesn't know how to get themselves safely back to the other side. Because we need to talk about that side too. It's there where we can get real lonely if we're not careful, if we're too quiet, if we believe the lie that we have to choose between the light and the dark and for some weird, broken reason deep inside of us, we must have chosen the black.

I kept my words inside far too long—and I regret it every single day—until they threatened to bubble up and over and couldn't be contained anymore and came out in a big rush of confessional honesty that was a lot like that recurring nightmare where you go out in public and realize, too late, that you are naked and everyone is staring. Also, speaking truth was the most freeing thing I'd ever done. It was both.

So yes, this: we can acknowledge that our one precious life is a gift and still stand up and say some parts of it kind of suck sometimes, and honestly, we probably should. And while there are still probably some people that would gnash their teeth at this and rail at me and say that we can't have it all, we can't be both sides of the coin at the same time, it's becoming harder and harder to hear them over the chorus of people who have raised their hands and said those two words that are the salve to almost any wound of loneliness: "Me too." And truthfully, I can't help but feel sorry for the people who insist on a life of black and white, because how ugly would it be to miss out on all the technicolor glory of a regular messy life lived in the regular messy in between of both.

And while I don't pretend for a second to know why these things happened to me or to any of us, why some things are given and others are taken away, what I do know for sure is that it's all connected: death and birth and loss and all of the things we pull into our chest and hold there for comfort and all of the things we have to let go of. If you cracked our chests open right now and all our pieces—the broken and the whole, the good and the bad, and even the ones we tried to hide—spilled out of us the way my mother's laugh spilled out of her mouth, it would make the most incredibly beautiful rainbow. And when enough time passes that we can take a few steps back, in just the right light with just the right distance, the vibrant colors of our lives will paint the kind of picture that reminds us of the breathtaking beauty there is to be found here in between the black and the white.

So what's at the end of my rainbow? Is my mother's struggle also my fate? I don't know, of course I don't. But I hope my story isn't even close to over yet. Let's just say I'm cautiously optimistic, at least today. But also scared; life is going to be hard sometimes. I might still break. I might, again, need medication, and there's not a single ounce of shame in that. I can't fathom a future where I won't need more therapy, and I need family and friends and community too to lift me up when I fall. Because I will fall. I know this, even as the edges of the grief start to dull and happiness glitters when the light hits it just right. But I will get back up. And for today, I can exist in the space between the hope and the fear. There is room in me for both.

Tomorrow remains to be seen, but here's hoping the colors are beautiful.

10

---◇---

The Butterfly and the Box of Teeth

"I just want to hit something!" Gabby hisses at me through the space in her mouth where her first two baby teeth have recently fallen out.

She is holding the closest object she could grab—conveniently, her brother's baseball bat—tightly in her chubby fingers, poised for the strike. Her feet are spread, belly and butt thrust out, shoulders back in righteous wild-child indignation. Her stance is half tiny ballerina, half Athena the warrior goddess. I find myself torn between scooping her up in my arms and running away from her as fast as I can.

I can remember when those teeth she'd lost came in too, the same first ones, tiny and white and precious. I have them and all the ones her brother and sister lost before her in a wooden box next to my bed. It's the same wooden box my mother kept next to her bed with *our* teeth in it—mine and my sisters—one of the few relics from my childhood I actually still have. Now all the teeth are all mixed in there together, mine and my sister's and my kids, with no way to know whose is whose, and Nick says I'm a little weird for keeping them like I have but they are staying right there, thank you very much. I like the symbolism of it, all of them jumbled up in there together in my box, that was my mother's box, that was before I bought it for her just a cheap trinket on the shelves of a souvenir shop on my first sleepaway school trip when I was in eighth grade.

Gabby didn't know my mother, not in the way I would have liked her to. She wasn't even born yet when my mother had mostly disappeared; fading into the space she spent the last few years of her life lost in. Gabby had turned three just a few weeks before my mom died, and my mother swore up and down she would show up for Gabby's spaghetti and meatballs birthday dinner and then—in a development that surprised none of us but Gabby—hadn't. After I had tucked the freshly three-year-old girl into bed that night and kissed the cake frosting from her forehead, I'd gone back downstairs to find that she'd left greasy handprints outlined in spaghetti sauce on the front windows where she must have stood, watching for her grandmother to arrive.

And that had made me that same kind of angry, the spitting-fire kind, the grab-a-baseball-bat kind. I wasn't angry at Gabby, not even as I scrubbed away her sauce prints, but at my mother or maybe at God or maybe at myself for the small part of me that had still, even though it was dumb, willed my mother to surprise us all and walk through the door.

As for Gabby, I'm not even sure what she is mad about, standing there with that bat in her hands. There was a toy, or more accurately, there wasn't. Someone had taken it from her, or she had lost it, or it hadn't been hers in the first place and she had only wanted it to be. I'm not sure it matters. What matters is that like me, she's a feeler, with a very thin filter between her heart and her actions. But that's where the similarity ends for us. Even though she's young, she's already one of those people who is always a little bit on fire, like there's a pilot light lit inside of her all the time and sometimes the wind blows just right and she flares up in a big showy rush of baseball-bat-grabbing heat. Even when she sleeps she's hot embers, always moving and never completely safe to be too close to.

It hasn't always been easy between us. Gabby doesn't need me in the same elemental way her sister and brothers do, and our temperaments are about as opposite as these things can come. At first, I wondered how I would do this. What can I possibly teach this girl about the world when the world she lives in is so vastly different than the world I'm from? She lets me take the bat from her though, and instead of running away I opt for the scooping, carrying her up into her bed and then lying there with her. Neither of really knows what to say so we're quiet for a while, the only noise our rush of breath. Mine is quick from carrying her weight up the stairs; hers is ragged with the remnants of cooling anger and a little whistle-y as it moves through her teeth hole.

"You know there are other ways, healthier ways, to deal with your anger," I tell her.

"Like what?"

"Like taking a deep breath," I say. And we practice, the drawing in, the pause, the release. It never fails to amaze me how much this simple platitude-sounding suggestion actually works, and we do it again and again together until we are both soft and a little bit melted into each other there on the bed. And then, in the stillness we've created, she asks me one of those Gabby questions, the kind that can't be answered in any real way but I try anyway because I am stubborn or because I love her or because I can remember myself what it felt like to ask someone the big questions, my mother or God, and not get any real answers.

"Why can't we keep things?"

I don't think she means it in a philosophical way, not on purpose anyway. I think she's probably talking about that toy, whatever trinket had been taken away from her and inspired her wrath in the first place. Or maybe she means her teeth. Or maybe, although probably not, she means her grandmother, because of course that's where my brain goes immediately.

What I don't tell her is how I'd thought I was losing her once, when she was little still and suddenly stopped breathing. She'd been sick, had a scary-high fever that had spiked quickly and out of nowhere, and I was laying down with her on my chest waiting for the medicine to bring it back down into more manageable territory. It took me a second even to realize that she wasn't breathing: first there was just nothing, the absence of sound, and then her soft baby body went unnaturally hard and stiff. Before my brain even caught up with my hands, I was on the phone with 911 and could hear the sirens in the background, racing towards our house.

She was back by the time the EMTs arrived at the door, soft again and breathing almost normal. It was a febrile seizure, they told me after examining her, no big deal but scary as all hell, and actually more common than you would think. This one was her first but she went on to have more, and they never stopped terrifying me in that primal way that leaves you shaken and with an adrenaline hangover for days afterward.

She'd stayed sick for a week after that first seizure, just a virus but a nasty enough one. When her fever broke finally on a surprisingly warm spring weekend morning, we collectively spilled outside like a group of weary hibernators starved for sunshine. I'd looked around, letting my eyes adjust to the light, and saw something move in the back corner by the shed. The lawn was that electric green it turns in the first few breaths of spring, but there was a dark spot in it. I moved closer and heard a sound like the cry of a baby. It was a kitten, a few days old maybe at most, curled up and tiny with its eyes closed and a hint of an umbilical cord still attached. Its mother was long gone, maybe scared off by our dog or our kids or our general chaotic volume level, and the abandoned kitten was in rough shape. I scooped it up from the grass.

"For the love of all that is temporary, do not get attached," I told myself, knowing this tiny, curled up, fit-in-your-palm of a thing didn't have a chance, but it was already too late. I knew this baby kitten was probably going to die, but I also knew I couldn't let it die alone in my backyard.

So I carried it inside in my palm like an offering, settled into the couch and held it against my chest while the sounds of my finally-healthy brood playing outside floated in through the open window. It held on for a while—long enough that I felt hope start to plant seeds in my heart—and then stopped breathing. Much like with Gabby, it took me a little while to realize anything had happened, and even longer this time to accept it. When I finally stood up, tears were streaming down my face, and I could hardly breathe myself. Lost, I called my mother.

"Mom," I managed to spit out in between my sobs, "I don't know why I am so upset. I don't even like cats."

She was quiet for a minute, long enough for me to doubt my decision to call her. It was stupid of me to think she would understand. But then she surprised me. "Liz," she said, "where was that kitten when it died?"

"On my chest," I answered, hesitant. Where was she going with this? Was she drunk?

"And where was Gabby when she had her seizure?"

All the breath I had struggled to find came out in a rush when I made the connection. "Oh. She was on my chest too."

I don't tell Gabby this story because I don't want to scare her, but also because I haven't yet made sense of it all, why some things need to be let go of and others come back and others you realize only later were never even yours to begin with.

Instead, I answer her with a different story, one of my favorites. I tell her how many years before, when her daddy and I were new parents, we took Jack for a walk in his stroller. I tell her too how it had been one of those gorgeous days in the fall where you know your communion with the sun is now on borrowed time and so everything feels a little extra bit like a gift, and while life with a new marriage and a new baby was incredibly hard a lot of the time, right then it felt full of promise.

We had hiked up the summit of the reservoir's water tower, where you could see the whole city and also the dot of white siding that was our own little house. "Look baby!" Nick and I had said, pointing. "It's our house!" Jack, being a baby, said nothing, although knowing him as well as I do now, I suspect he was thinking something snarky about how it takes a special kind of idiot to walk all this way just to turn around and look for home.

Just then a butterfly had flown by, and operating on a lark or instinct, Nick reached out his hand and, surprising us both, caught it. He held his hand out to me, an expression of disbelief on his face. In his loosely clenched fingers I could see the flap of the butterfly's wings. "No way," I said. "You caught it?"

"Yup," he said, and then looked from his hand to me again. "So now what?"

"Well, now I think you have to let it go," I said, because clearly it was the only thing he *could* do; it wouldn't be fair to him or the butterfly for him to keep it caged up in his fist. So he opened his hand back up and eventually, after it had recovered from the daze and realized it was free, the butterfly flew away. Jack squealed his little baby squeal as it flew past, and we headed back towards the white dot that was home.

I tell Gabby how maybe it is always like that butterfly. Maybe, if we are lucky, we catch something and we draw it close to us, marvel at its beauty and marvel even more at the gift that is us holding it. But we can't hold it forever, and not just because it would be awkward if we did, but because in doing so eventually we would destroy the very thing that made the moment beautiful in the first place: its inevitable ending.

Gabby listens intently. There's no way she is going to get this, I tell myself, for no other real reason than I haven't exactly got it all myself. But I'm always underestimating her. "Also," she says, "if your hands were always full of butterfly, you wouldn't be able to hold onto anything else."

Which is kind of everything, isn't it?

It's the teeth, pushing up and into my baby's mouth until they come out again and into my box. It's me giving my mother the box in the first place, only to have the box then given back to me when she died. It's her, here and then not. It's having babies and then not having babies anymore but having these children, these people who can stand on their own, feet slightly spread and fingers holding a bat in my kitchen, lit like flames with anger that is caught, held, and then released later when she surrenders back into my arms. It's my own anger at my mother, long since burned through into grief and love and even something that looks a lot like peace.

It's at its most basic just the ebb and flow of Gabby's soft breath, the inhale of all the things we pull in and hold close, flowing into the exhale of all the things we have no real choice but to release and set free.

And it's what came not that long after the fire calmed back into embers and we'd gone back about our lives, the baseball bat safely put away. We had been sitting together, Gabby and me, entwined on the couch watching TV or reading a book, I don't exactly remember. What I remember is that she had shifted somehow in my arms just right, and for a second it was there, the smell of my mother's perfume, clear as day and unmistakably hers. "My mother is here," I said out loud before I had time to realize what a weird thing it was to say to a child. And Gabby leapt up out of my arms and ran to the door, threw it open. "Come in, come in, come in!" she had yelled, joyous instead of the freaked out I'd expected her to be. "I've been waiting for you."

It was the kind of moment you wanted to hold onto for a little while, sad but also beautiful, and I was glad by then that I had let go of enough to have some space inside my heart for it.

11

---◊---

The Happiest Day
of My Life

Every year, as far back as I can remember, my mother told me my birth story on my birthday. Every year, that is, except the last one, the year I turned thirty-four, the year I was absurdly pregnant with my fourth baby, the year—two days after my birthday—that she killed herself. It had always been one of my very favorite traditions and even though I knew things were bad that last birthday eve, I had half-expected my phone to ring anyway.

"When you were born, it was the happiest day of my life . . ." was how it always started, which was funny because the actual birth sounded kind of awful. She'd been in labor for a total of three days, took no drugs, and by the end was full-on hallucinating that she was a cast member on the then-popular show *Dallas*.

When I got pregnant for the first time, I'd asked her what to expect, truly, and the only advice she gave me was to take all the drugs you are offered. Which I did, happily, for my first three births. And they'd been fine, honestly, thankfully. There were no complications and no horror stories, which meant the birth stories I told my own kids were less eventful. I'd give them little details mixed in there to make them laugh, like how Jack was covered in fine black hair all over his little body when he was born or how at one point when I was in labor with Maria I took a bath, and my midwife and Nick and my mother and sister—my birth team—got so engrossed in a conversation about local real estate in the other room that they forgot where I was.

Or I would tell Gabby about how she came out completely ravenous, how she sucked on anything and everything: the doctor's stethoscope, her father's finger, my necklace, air. It makes sense, if you knew her now, that she was this way then. What I don't tell her is how in the weeks after she was born, as she grew and continued to consume life in big hungry gulps, the opposite happened to me. I became flatter and duller. I was tired all the time, sure, but this was that bone-aching tired that sleep doesn't come close to touching. I was anxious too, terri-fied that I was screwing her up or about to screw her up, and then thoughts started to creep in, uninvited, from the edges of the darkness: maybe they would be better off without me.

I asked my doctor at the time, "Could this be postpartum depression? After my third kid? Does that even happen?"

He said, and I quote, "I'm not sure what you want me to do here. I'm not a psychologist." It had taken courage for me to speak up, and this dismissal made me feel like I was being erratic, self-indulgent, or maybe just hormonal. He did send me home with a prescription for antidepressants, but with no counsel. Would I have to stop nursing to take them? Was it worth it? I sat up late that night with this prescription in my hand, and I worried if taking them was the wrong choice.

You see what I'm saying, right? I didn't know. Nick didn't know either. We had two children already and we thought the third would be easy. I'd been pregnant three times, was raising three little kids, and thought I knew what there was to know about motherhood. But this? No one told me. No one said I could love my baby so much and still wonder if I had made a huge mistake. No one told me you could feel broken and battered and bent under the weight of sadness and anxiety and yet seemingly still look normal enough that it would surprise people when you scared yourself enough to weakly raise your voice and ask for help.

No one told me I would spend my evenings after everyone else had gone to bed, lifting my third baby's sleeping form from her crib and just holding her against me, resting my weeping head in her nest of curls, whispering, "I'm so sorry, baby. I'm just so sorry."

No one told me that yes, you can get postpartum depression with your third baby after not having it with the first two. And no one told me that taking the pills was the absolute right choice, but somehow by the grace of something I took them anyway, and they helped.

I still don't know what it was about that third birth that was different. Maybe it was how my mother wasn't there. She'd been there for Jack and Maria's births but was too unreliable by the time Gabby was born, and when labor hit Nick and I had snuck off to the hospital in the middle of the night all by ourselves. Things had progressed slowly and when the epidural kicked in, Nick dozed next to me in the chair and I watched the moon out of the hospital window, trying to sleep but not succeeding. The medicine was on a pump that I controlled, and I'd accidentally given myself too much. I couldn't feel anything, which you would think would be a relief but instead was weird, disconcerting and unnatural. The contractions would come and there would be tightness but no pain, just an uncomfortableness and a sense of melancholy that was out of place for such a happy occasion. But the birth was easy, and the baby was healthy and perfect and spunky, even if I wasn't.

And while I knew all along—even as I was fighting to pull myself out of the trenches of the PPD—that I wanted a fourth baby, I was terrified now in a way I never had been before. We debated for a long time whether or not the risk was worth it and spent a good while looking into adoption as well, but in the end I knew I had to trust my body again. When I found out I was pregnant with our fourth, I vowed to do everything differently. I found a new midwife and made plans to give birth at home, no drugs, surrounded by my family. The pregnancy was healthy, and I took great care of myself and did everything right, and then, three weeks before the due date (and two days after my birthday), my mother died.

Every single day after that, I was absolutely sure I would go into labor. Isn't that how shock works? All I thought about—all day long—was having the baby. We planned my mother's funeral and I helped pick out the right hymns and bought church-worthy clothes for the kids, but the entire time I was silently begging him to come out, maintaining a steady plea directly from my heart to my uterus, willing my labor to start. I knew I was going to have that baby any second, I had to, it was the only thing that made any sense anymore.

I remembered being in labor with Jack, lying strapped to monitors on the hospital bed, my mother holding my hand with her eyes on the display screen. At the beginning of every contraction, before the pain came, there would be a spike in the reading, and she would say, "Okay, here it comes." I'd squeeze her hand, tensing my whole body against the pain that I knew was coming. This was like that, except I was stuck in the waiting stage. I was tensed, as ready as I could be, waiting for something that wouldn't come. What I didn't realize until later, of course, was that all that tensing I was doing was probably keeping my body from doing what it would have done naturally, had I been able to relax and let it, had I not been completely terrified.

And even when it did happen, after my due date had come and gone, I wasn't ready. Labor started fast and furious when it did finally start, and I tried to pretend it wasn't happening, told no one I was having contractions at all, and snuck off upstairs by myself to take a warm bath and see if I could slow things down. I was definitely not in labor, I told myself. I just wanted to be alone. The usual.

The hot water felt good on my sore back. I stretched my legs out over the edge and tried to relax, but in the bathtub the contractions quickly got much stronger. They were coming one on top of the other with no space in between to even stop, breathe, collect myself. Ten minutes had gone by, or maybe it was an hour. I couldn't tell. The pain was incredible, almost too much, and panic started to set in. I wasn't going to be able to do this after all, I realized. I tried to take it all back, all of the wanting and wishing that labor would hurry up. I could stay pregnant forever, I rationalized. The baby was safer inside. I was safer that way too. Because this wasn't what was supposed to happen, I thought. It hurt so badly, and the pain came every thirty seconds or so and lasted minutes at a time. There was no relief, no place to listen to the playlist I had made or light the candles I had bought or consult the detailed birth plan I'd made. I can't do this, I said, over and over. I can't do this. *I cannot do this.*

And then it stopped for a moment, just like that, the pain gone and in its place, light. I smelled my mother's perfume and knew she was with me, as crazy as that sounds. She'd hallucinated in labor that she was a cast member on *Dallas*; maybe I hallucinated that she was with me in my bathroom, I don't know. But something helped me to shift, to soften—maybe it was her, maybe it was the wisdom that had always been inside of me—and when the next contraction hit I was able to relax into it instead of tensing against it, and that made all the difference.

Because it is the only thing that works, and not just for contractions. It's all of it: grief and loss and PPD and all of the pain, everywhere. If we stand rigid against it, odds are it will sweep over us in a terrific rush and either swallow us whole or knock us down trying. But if we relax into it, if we accept it for what it is and try, even, to breathe, often we can ride the wave and come out the other side still mostly in one piece.

There was a pounding sound then which I thought maybe was my heartbeat. I stepped out of the bathtub and back into myself. The pulsing sound clarified into the insistent sound of someone knocking on the locked bathroom door. "Liz?" It was

Nick. Of course. "Are you in there? Are you okay?" I opened the door and fell to the bathroom floor. Nick caught me, and two pushes later, he caught our baby boy.

———◊———

The Buddha said life is suffering. I know this because Nick quotes it to me often, every time I complain about trivialities like him leaving the toilet seat up again or not shutting the kitchen cabinet all of the way or picking the crunchiest snack to eat right next to me while I am trying to watch my shows. He says it half-joking, just as I complained half-jokingly in the first place, but like everything important, there's a deep river of truth that runs through his words. And in many respects, I think he is right. So much of this life is suffering.

There is loss everywhere, the million small ones we live every day: the loss of the summer sun as we move into fall; the loss of the golden leaves falling from the tree outside as we lay in our bed together, now a family of six, the same family as we were before everything in some ways but different, too. Complete. And there are the big, unspeakable losses, like the loss of my mother, first in bits and pieces when she started to succumb to her illness and then in a final rush all at once when she took her life.

And maybe even the joys of this life contain suffering in them, I thought as I brushed the dusting of downy brown hair on my baby's head back from his forehead. There is all of the million discomforts of pregnancy, of carrying and growing a baby to term. There's the unbelievable pain of labor, of transition. And there is the pain of birth, of letting go.

It's easy too, if we're not careful, to get wrapped up in the suffering of these losses, to get stuck there, and to forget to see the joy. I know this because I have done it. Over and over again I have instinctively stiffened against the suffering, not realizing that in doing so I was making it worse. It was ingrained in me because it was the only way I knew how to keep going. I didn't want to let myself feel it because I was afraid if I did, I wouldn't come back. I was afraid I would have followed my mother.

But grief, like labor, is like life: if you stiffen yourself against it, you are only prolonging the inevitable. Because here's the thing: it is coming anyway, and if you are stiff enough it will knock you down and sweep you away in its path. Sooner or later, the stiffening that you did as a matter of survival will threaten to be the very thing that kills you, and the only real thing you can do to stay alive is to soften and find a way to believe that you will come out the other side.

I laid awake that night long after everyone else had fallen asleep. The baby, who we named Luca, slept on my chest, his skin against mine and my robe wrapped around the both of us. Nick had brought me a beer earlier, to help the milk come in he'd said, but really I think it was so we could toast each other. "To Luca," he'd said as the glasses clinked.

"To us," I said. The beer sat half-empty on the bedside table next to me, and I watched as condensation dripped down the side of the brown bottle. I had tried to finish it but couldn't. For once, there just didn't seem to be room inside of me for anything else. I was full.

The baby stirred, and I pushed the blankets back to stand up and get a clean diaper. After I changed him, he was restless, or maybe I was, so we walked together in circles through the house, eventually ending up back in the bathroom. I rocked him back and forth, dancing that instinctive dance that millions of mothers had danced before me, including mine.

Luca's eyes, the same exact shade of deep blue that my mother's had been, were open and he watched my face as I spoke to him, starting a tradition that I hoped would last a very long time. "When you were born," I began, "it was the happiest day of my life."

12

———◊———

The Witching Hour

For a long time, there was an unfinished plastered-over patch of wall in the girls' bedroom that mocked me. It was from some work we had done where I breezily said to the wanting-to-go-home contractor, "Oh, sure, I can take care of that last bit, no worries. Get outta here!" Easy peasy lemon squeezy.

And yet I didn't, of course, because who has time for that kind of shit? And so every time I walked by there, every time I saw it and remembered how I had to fix it and how it had been there quite some time and I hadn't done it yet and likely wouldn't, not for a long time anyway, my inner voice would unleash a scathing monologue on my inadequacies as a housekeeper and mother and general human being, and I hated myself a little more. You know this voice—maybe not this one, exactly, this lovely combination of my mother's voice and the worst, whiniest, version of myself and a little bit of Fran

Drescher when she's overtired—but your own personal version of it, the one that sounds like nails on a chalkboard on a good day and is considerably less easy to keep at bay when it feels like the whole world is falling apart or things are not getting *handled*. My voice asks me things constantly, things that don't really need or expect an answer, questions designed to remind me that no matter how decent my hair looks or how many times I get the kids to school almost on time that there will be more, always, waiting for me to do.

And my voice, of course, is at her loudest and most nasal in the middle of the night when I can't sleep, which is way too often. Like my mother before me, I have struggled with insomnia my whole life. I've spent many a night lying awake in the dark after everyone else has fallen into the peace of a deep sleep, listening to the voice barrage me with her most important questions, things like:

"Are you really just going to lie there?"

"Did you actually need that third taco?"

"Whatever happened to medical school?"

"Is that a whisker?"

If I was a better person, I would look at insomnia as a gift, or at least a sign that God–Mary–Mom (the catchall who I pray to these days) was listening when I whined that there just wasn't enough time in the day. And if I was an even better person than that, I would actually use those hours to accomplish important and oft-neglected things like toilet cleaning and meal prepping, although not necessarily in that order. Except I'm pretty much the worst version of my already crappy self at three o'clock in the morning, so instead of being positive or productive, I usually decide to spend the time staring at the ceiling, fighting an ever-increasing sense of panic and reflecting on every poor decision I have ever made in my life (like that time when I was eight and I cut my eyebrows off with my mother's manicure scissors), while wondering how one could live in a house filled to the brim with people and still feel so incredibly alone.

Because that's what the darkness does, isn't it? It takes us when we are at our worst—the makeup long removed and our hair a little birds-nest-esque from hours spent tossing and turning, and maybe I shouldn't even call your attention to the granny panties that are a little floppy since they lost their elastic a few hundred washes ago—and it throws us deep into the scariest parts of our minds with nary a hand to pull us out because everyone else is sleeping. This, my friends, is what my mother used to call the witching hour.

Not only is it dark out there during this witching hour, but it's the inky kind of dark that makes us doubt the certainty of the sun ever actually rising again. And our families are in the enviable phase of sleep where their breath has slowed enough to compel us—in our vulnerable state—to keep putting our hands on their chests to make sure they are not dead. It's silly really, but that is exactly what I'm talking about. Who does that shit in the normal light of day? Could you imagine sitting in a meeting at work next to a guy who has been quiet for so long that you convince yourself he might actually be dead? I spent a lot of years working in the public sector where people actually did sleep at work, and I still never felt compelled to put my hand on their chests. This is the kind of stuff that only makes sense when it's the witching hour.

It's in the witching hour too that we are most vulnerable to the stories that our voice tells. "You're not good enough," it says, and we nod our bedraggled heads along agreeably, because what kind of decent person cuts off their eyebrows with manicure scissors, anyway? "You will never have enough," is another common witching hour refrain, whatever "it" be: money, love, romance, ice cream, pain relief, forgiveness, time, or just plain old sleep. It's easy then in the dark to forget how everything we need is right inside of us anyway, always was. The witching hour is like those terrible sunglasses they make you wear after you have a procedure done on your eyes, the ones that dim the lights and block out everything but what's right in front of your face so you can't see all of the people walking alongside of you. It's easy to look out the window through the dim lenses and into that inky black and think about how everyone else must be doing it better than you. For sure they are sleeping, and not making a mental list of all of the terrible things they said to their mother when they were angry that it's now too late to ever take back.

But then inevitably I'll wake up, having fallen asleep sometime there in the midst of trying to convince myself that we had sandpaper somewhere in the basement and I really should just get up and fix the wall already, and it would be the chaos of morning, and there it would go again, forgotten or at least remembered but ignored. That is, until I took a week off from work and I just knew everything was going to change. I was full of time-off dreams and resolutions: I will clean! I will exercise! I will cook! I will wear pants most days! And of course, the most important one: I will fix the wall.

Instead, I got sick. It started with the flu—or so I thought—fever and body aches and a sense of impending doom so bad that I sat on the couch wrapped in blankets and wept for no real reason other than I needed to. I tried to rest and figured it would go away on its own, but it didn't, and soon I had nerve pain in my hands and feet that was so terrible it took my breath away. "You should go to the doctor," Nick said after days of watching me cry and whine and not change my sweatpants.

"We've got time!" I yelled back, giving Nick the same answer I'd always say automatically back to the inner voice as it barraged me with a to-do list too long for any actual human to accomplish in one lifetime. We've got time. But time went by and I stayed sick. I started to pray a little, asking God–Mary–Mom to give me a sign that everything would be okay. God–Mary–Mom responded by making a dead monarch butterfly fall out of the sky in front of me as I finally walked myself into my doctor's office. On the way home, after plenty of blood tests and no answers, the radio played Glenn Frey's "The Heat Is On," and my fever pulsed along to the beat, and I followed a company van with a skull and crossbones painted on the back. "That's enough with the signs, you guys," I told God–Mary–Mom, and when we got home I laid on the floor to try to get my bearings. Luca asked for milk, and I said, "In a minute, Baby. We've got time."

But we didn't. My doctor called shortly after. My white blood cell count was too low, she said. I needed to be hospitalized immediately, a pronouncement which made me burst into tears in front of God–Mary–Mom and my kids. This was when we started to get scared, the voice and me. She doesn't do unknowns well; things get a little screechy. We have this in common. "But I have so much to do," we yelled in perfect harmony. I passed by the wall as I packed an overnight bag for the hospital, let my fingers brush the unfinished plaster dust from the edges of the hole. We have time, I tried, but it came out as a question.

It turns out there are perks to having a low white blood cell count in the hospital. They don't make you wait in the waiting room and you are pretty much guaranteed a private room, where I sat alone while doctors and nurses paraded in and out, running more tests and becoming more agitated.

"I have this terrible pain in my feet," I said to one doctor, who was getting kind of desperate.

"Let me see them," he answered, and I warned him that it had been a while since my last pedicure and they were kind of gross.

"I've seen it all," he reassured me, and I took my socks off.

"Hmm."

"What?"

"You're right. They *are* gross."

The voice, which had been quiet for a while, laughed. I did too.

Later he poked me so hard in the belly that I grimaced, so he declared right then and there that I must have an abdominal infection and sent me off for a cat scan. There was no abdominal infection. My chest X-ray was suspicious and needed to be redone because the radiologist was convinced I had a foreign body implanted into my rib. It was the snap from my hospital gown. In short, no one actually knew what was wrong with me.

When I had had enough radiation to emit a soft glow and we still had no answers, I was admitted. They pumped me full of IV antibiotics and fluids and when I was comfy and beeping from places I didn't know could beep, they sent another doctor in. She was a hematologist-oncologist (blood cancer doctor, she said, when I looked at her wide-eyed and uncomprehending) and young and cute, right down to her high-heeled shoes, which made me feel extra ugly in my ratty gown and two-day makeup. She talked for a while, but I stopped listening after she said *cancer,* the breath stuck in my throat. This wasn't an answer or a diagnosis, I heard her say. Just a conversation that needed to happen, because the more things we ruled out the better chance that it was cancer.

I stared at her heels. "So that just happens?" I asked her, when she finished. "People just get leukemia? At thirty-six?"

She nodded slowly. "Yes, it happens."

When she left the room I started to google "survival rates of blood cancers" on my phone, but I couldn't really see well because my eyes were teary and I had left the harsh hospital overhead lights off all day because my self-esteem can only take so much. I put my phone down and laughed at how stupid we were, my inner voice and me. Because all of her questions in the end didn't matter; of course they didn't. And my answer, my go-to mantra of motherhood and survival, was, "We've got time." Well, it was inherently flawed because it's not always true, we don't always have the time we think we have. Sometimes we wake up one morning and things have changed and our lives will forever from that point on be unrecognizable to who we used to be, that cocky woman who thought there was nothing more important than a clean countertop and a nice number on the scale. Sometimes we wake up and our mother is gone, and we are sick and everything is changing so much that you can feel yourself physically being wrenched out of the rhythm of the life you've known and thrown into something different, like being tossed into the deep end of a pool and trying to figure out where the bottom is and if you can swim and how long, in the end, do you have before you're too tired to do it anymore.

The voice still asked questions there in the darkness because some habits are so deeply ingrained that even the biggest changes can't touch them, God–Mary–Mom bless it, but they were softer, things like: What would you do, Liz, with your time, if you knew it was running out?

Would you still stand in front of the mirror in the morning, cursing your lines and your lumps?

Or would you pen a love letter to yourself in eyeliner you had just used for the last time, thanking this incredible vessel for carrying you through it all in one piece?

Would you let it all get in and under your skin, the weather, the traffic, the internet trolls? Would you let your precious breath continue to shorten with every perceived inconvenience until you were panting your way through your finite minutes?

Or would you suddenly notice the way the sunlight reflects off the snow or the blacktop or a forgotten shiny red tricycle and realize how you'd been making your way through your days with your eyes half shut for as long as you could remember?

Would you keep hiding from everyone you knew, ducking behind grocery store displays and into alleyways in an attempt to hide your less-than-perfect hair day or to avoid awkward small talk?

Or would your face light up at the familiar faces, arms as open as your heart had been thrown? Would you listen when they told you how they were? Would you suggest coffee, a hug?

Would you connect?

Would you answer the phone?

Would you soften into your husband's touch instead of shying away?

Would you ask for more time?

And if you had it, what would you do differently?

Later, the blood cancer doctor came back with her boss, a quiet, older man. He made eye contact with me right away and was wearing sensible shoes, and I loved him instantly. He told me that I was being released. Something they'd given me was working, it seemed. My white blood cell count had started to rebound. "So . . ." I started, afraid to ask the obvious. "It's not leukemia?"

"Go home," he said. "Get some rest. We will answer that question in a few days. I'll make you an appointment at the cancer center."

And so I left the next day, arms bruised in all the places they stuck me with needles. "Can I drive myself home?" I asked Nurse Desiree as she wheeled me out.

She didn't know, she said, no one had ever done that before.

"Well then I'm gonna be your first," I told her, and she wheeled me to the door and I got up and walked to my car and drove away. The sun was brilliant and I felt better than I had in a week, even though there were no answers and I was staring down the scariest possibility I had faced yet. I let the warmth of the natural light wash over me, and as it did I remembered something I'd forgotten in the chaos and delirium of the past few days. The night before I'd gone to the doctor and then the hospital, the last night where I tossed and turned in the inky black of the witching hour, wrestling with both my pain and my demons, I'd turned onto my side, facing the window next to my side of the bed, and seen, out of the corner of my eye and partially blocked by the curtain, a flickering light.

When I'd pulled the curtain back, I saw it was a candle in the neighbor's window. If I laid still and put my head just right on the pillow I could watch it, and I did, for hours. I was sick and scared of what was going to happen; all my grief and sadness and inadequacy wanted to rush over me in a witching-hour tidal wave, but I anchored myself so tightly to that light in the window and I didn't let go, no matter what. I think this is what hope looks like, I decided that afternoon. It doesn't have to be much and it doesn't even have to be ours; it can be the light of a candle in someone else's window, even. It's just a matter of finding the bright spot in the darkness and hanging on as tight as we can to it so we don't get swallowed up.

I drove myself to my cancer center appointment a few days later too, where I was sitting and waiting to be seen when my doctor's office called. It wasn't cancer, they said. My Lyme disease test had come back positive. I wept with relief. Lyme is a serious disease, but it's manageable. I believed then that this diagnosis was a gift. It was the time I had asked God–Mary–Mom for.

What I realized later though, as I tried to settle into a life that had changed, a life where I now had a disease that may or may not ever go away, a life where I found myself in bed more often than I cared to admit, rocked with the exhaustion and pain that is Lyme's trademark, was that the whole experience had been a gift. I'm still here, sure, but I'm different. A few days in the darkness of that hospital, staring down my own mortality, had shifted my perspective in a real way. My inner voice and I had a lot of time to talk it out there while we waited, and we had been able to make a truce. She still harasses me, sure, but her voice never lost that softness it had acquired there in the hospital, and her reminders are tinged with the realization that some things don't really matter, not in the end (like clean countertops and patched-up walls), and some things do.

I did eventually patch up the wall. I didn't do the best job though, and you can still see the outline of where the hole was, where the seams of the patch lie against the smoothness of the original wall. Before Lyme, this obviousness would have driven me and the voice crazy, but now, it has kind of grown on me. It feels like a very accurate representation of the life we are making here in this house and in this world. A patched-up, imperfect, gorgeous life that is, after all, completely temporary. We have only the time we have, this much I know for sure. What we do with it is what matters. And I'll be damned if I'm going to waste any more of it torturing myself with silly regret.

Ain't nobody got time for that.

13

———◇———

If It Was Only Ever This

I did an interview recently where the interviewer asked me a question I've been asked before and always trip over: "So, Liz, what is your ultimate goal?"

I assume he meant writing-wise, since that was the interview subject, but it wasn't specifically stated, and I had to put a hand over my mouth to keep from shouting random goals out into the universe, like financial independence, bigger boobs, a faster split pace when I run, a walk-in closet, children who listen to what I say the first time I say it, the secret to my best friend's killer lemon bar recipe, or maybe a car from the last five years.

I read the other day that you do most of your living in the first twenty years of your existence and the rest of it is just trying to process that living. I don't know yet if this is the most depressing thing I have ever heard or if it's a giant relief, but either way, I'm pretty sure it's horseshit. Regardless, it gave me pause, because what I do know is that there is this very real turning point, right about where I am now in my thirties, where a life is no longer about the planning for and moving towards and reaching for, but instead is about the right now.

And maybe it didn't turn out the way you wanted it to. It's hard to even say that, isn't it? Because I do believe that the way it turned out–*is* turning out–is exactly the way it was *supposed* to turn out, but that doesn't mean it turned out the way I had dreamed it would when it was all out in front of me, and I was six years old and my Mom gave me a copy of the constitution and I read the whole thing while sitting on the toilet. I got so excited back then when I saw that nowhere in that whole thing did it say I couldn't be president just because I had a vagina and ran out to tell her the news without even remembering to pull my pants up. I had *plans*, you guys. Big ones.

But it's been eons since then, and so many of my very own best choices–like to marry young and start a family and to have all the babies that my heart cried out for–mean that other things just don't fit, not the way I thought they would when I was young and made all those plans that the unceasing march of time has pulled from me so slowly and sneakily that I couldn't have seen it happening even if I tried. This life is hopefully not even close to over yet, but it's probably safe to say I will not get the chance to be a Fly Girl on *In Living Color* or become a surgeon or discover how to time travel, and not just so I can go back and break up with my high school boyfriend before he breaks up with me. I still don't know how to garden, even, and I've wanted to learn how to cook authentic Mexican food for over a decade, yet I haven't evolved past melting a whole mess of shredded cheese on a flour tortilla, heating it up in the microwave, and calling it a taco. It's pathetic.

But I've done the big milestone things I set out to do, despite some serious challenges. I graduated from high school, and then from college. I had my babies, I married my husband, I bought my house. I have a career that I love and a hobby I love even more. The work of the getting is starting to be behind me and I'm (mostly) ready to do the work of the having. And you would think this would be the easy part, except in many ways it's not.

Who knew? Why would this, the part of life where we can settle into the choices we've made and stop agonizing over what the next big step needs to be, be the hardest yet? All that looking forward should have been hard, and it was, but it was that exquisite kind of hard that's wrought with expectation and promise. This is, well, what it is. And maybe what happens is that the looking forward becomes the looking inward, and we notice that even with all of the joy and all of the chaos and all of the living we are busy doing, the longing is still there.

So yes, I'm going to say it. There were dreams bigger than this, bigger dreams than standing here knee-deep in laundry with a saggy tummy and early onset wrinkle-face and the soft but unsilenceable voice inside that also remembers what it felt like to run yelling through the upstairs hallway bare-butted and waving that faux parchment constitution around like it was my flag, telling my mama how I was going to change the world. And yet I'm the one who traded them away, aren't I? I set those dreams down willingly and of my own accord in a deal so stacked in my favor that if I had the nerve to even think about complaining about it for even a second, I'd have to punch my own self in the face.

So I'm not complaining. I'm not. All I'm saying is that it's not fair that we keep perpetuating this myth that we can have it all. It's not fair and it's not true. We can't have it all, not really. No one can. We can have incredible, beautiful, amazing things. We can have big, huge, even satisfying pieces of lots of things. If you're way luckier than you deserve to be, like I was, you might even have a mother-in-law who is the physical embodiment of grace and watches your children while you carve yourself out a career that still feels mostly fulfilling most of the time. But even with them in her capable hands, a piece of me was never exactly able to leave my kids, not all the way, which means I wasn't fully present at work. And back at home, one ear and eye on call with my smart phone next to me, I wasn't fully present for the wiping or the feeding or the story reading on the other side. We do that, don't we? We consciously split ourselves in half or thirds or further, into teeny little pieces that we sprinkle over the parts of our life like fairy dust and pray that it will be enough to keep everyone, including us, satiated.

And is it? Here's the thing: I think so. I really do. It has to be. Because when we're little and dreaming big, no one tells us how much of life is just survival mode. They say it will be amazing (and it is!), and they say it will be hard (and it is!), and they say to lean in or dig deep, but no one really says how there can be whole stretches of time where you just have to hold on, a white-knuckled death grip the only thing standing between being here and drifting off like an untethered balloon towards madness or the heavens, same diff.

So yeah, I also think it's okay to grieve the loss of some of those old dreams. Life with littles is hard. It's a tightrope walk. We choose the things that we can carry and we try to accept the things that we can't, and we sweat and crawl and grip to stay on that rope and balance it all, and the truth is, it isn't easy and it isn't very glamorous, either. So as much as I would love to be, I'm not a Fly Girl or a surgeon. I'm a working, bedraggled mother to four babies, half in and half out, whose ultimate goal and crowning achievement most days is simply surviving to see another one.

Maybe that's why people seem to always stop when they see me with my four babies, stare, and say, although not unkindly, "Boy, you sure do have your hands full, don't you?" Or maybe it's the way I look most of the time, the slightly crazed and manic expression I wear on my face when I go out with all of them in public, the way my shoulders droop towards the ground with exhaustion. Or maybe it's that quite often my hands are literally full, piled high with snacks and drinks and crappy toys made out of plastic and discarded shoes and ponytail holders and piles and piles of garbage that for some unbeknownst reason must always be handed to me rather than just put into the receptacle designed explicitly for this purpose.

And like the question from the interviewer, I never know exactly how to answer this. Is it an actual question? "You sure do have your hands full, don't you?" I don't even know if it's meant to be an insult or a light-hearted observation or even a compliment, something very American-esque about how incredible I must be at multitasking if for no other reason than because I have clearly had unprotected sex at least four times. But I'm not good at multitasking, not at all. I'm not particularly good at any of this, not by a long shot, and honestly, you don't see me often out in public with all four of them. Because by the time evening rolls around and I'm done working and the children have been mostly fed and maybe wiped down, usually I am lying exhausted on the floor in my house with someone's poop or vomit on my shirt, trying to muster the strength to crawl towards the garbage can so I can dispose of the most recent gross thing that has been handed to me by a passing child. So yes, I guess you could say I have my hands full.

Thing is, we all do. Raising kids is hard. Maintaining a functional relationship is hard. Having a job, keeping a house livable, paying the bills, staying healthy, making time, finding enlightenment, living an everyday, messy, regular life: it's all hard, an awful lot of the time. Losing my mom on top of it all? So incredibly hard. Are there things that are harder? Absolutely. There are terrifically terrible things that happen to incredible people in this life, and if you sat for too long and tried to make sense of it all, it would break the hearts of even the strongest among us into little pieces next to me, where I lie on the floor.

But this isn't a hardness competition, and saying that this regular, everyday life is hard doesn't mean that other stuff isn't hard. Or harder. The hardest, maybe. Probably. I don't know for sure, because this feeling of living in the moment is the only life I know: this life with four children where I work and try hard to serve everything and everyone well, like my faith, husband, babies, job, friends, community, grief, the memory of my mother, and everything else, while accepting the truth that we simply cannot be amazing at everything. I want to be, believe me. I want to be so badly that it causes me physical pain to admit that I can't be. I want to line the edges up perfectly in every facet of my life, buff it all to a gleaming smudge-free shine, and tuck it all neatly into a freshly made bed every night, satisfied that I did my best. But I can't. This is not that life, not right now, not yet.

This is a life of making space for the most important things by carving and scratching and clawing.

It's a life of crawling sometimes and running others and half-assing almost everything.

It's catching up on email and doing my eye makeup and drinking my coffee while on the toilet.

It's promising my husband I will wake him up later after the kids are asleep so we can spend some time alone together only to wake up the next morning still in my work clothes with creases from the sofa permanently etched into the collagen-challenged skin of my face.

It's having to say no to people and places and events and to dreams and goals that I really want to say yes to, and accepting that the chance might not come around again. It's having to cancel other things at the last minute so many times that even the strongest friends will start to wonder if it's on purpose. It's almost always wondering if everyone is hanging out without me, and it's missing those friends with an ache and a need so real and raw that I'm half tempted to book an impromptu all-inclusive trip for all of us that I can't afford and leaves tomorrow.

But I can't. Not right now. Not yet.

Not yet, of course, being the refrain of the song of this life. Time alone with my husband? Not yet. A regular ladies night? Not yet. Finishing the book I've been writing for longer than

I'd care to admit? Not yet. Losing the baby weight? Not yet. Sleeping through the night? Not yet. Having a clean house? Not yet. Not yet. You get the idea.

It's a life of miraculous wonder too, and the real goal that I'm trying to make room for now is to not be so busy or distracted that I forget that. Because it's a life that by virtue of its chaos is passing so quickly that I want to grab it by the lapels and pull it down onto the ground with me and force it to slow down so I can both take a breath and maybe, for a second, fully appreciate its glorious beauty.

Because it's a life we would do all again, if given the choice, isn't it? If the Ghost of Christmas Past came blowing through right this second and took us on a journey backward, wouldn't we pick these very same people out of a long lineup of options, even if they were covered in dirt and scabs and food stains and had peanut butter smeared in their hair? Wouldn't we grab them all up in our hands and drag them home so fast we would just be a peanut-butter-scented-blur to passersby, and they would barely have time to take a second glance before calling out after us: "Boy, you sure do have your hands full, don't you?"

But I'd let the interviewer wait long enough. And eventually, after thinking for a second, I said what I'm pretty near certain is the truth: "If it was only ever this, just what I have right now and nothing more, then that would have been more than enough."

Part of me still struggles to admit this truth though, because of course I still have dreams, even if they're a little different now. You couldn't pay me enough to be president, to start. I hate blood and would have made a terrible surgeon, and I hear

Fly Girls keep terrible work hours. These days, my dreams are more along the line of achieving enlightenment or at least that elusive arm balance pose in yoga, and that's just today's edition. Yesterday's dream was to get out of bed in the morning and this weekend's is to watch a whole movie with my husband without having to get up from the couch once. Tomorrow, maybe, I will finally figure out what a tamale is, or save the world, depending on how much coffee I can stomach in the morning.

Just recently, I've been letting myself whittle away hours of insomnia, lying in bed and planning a book launch party attended by the likes of my new bestie Oprah, where waiters serve from big trays of bacon-wrapped everything, and I drink just enough from the open bar to have incredible dance moves, but not so much that I start pulling people aside and ugly crying about how much I love them. But that's just the stuff of silly dreams, and anyway, I don't think having dreams means I can't also appreciate the forest for the trees. I'm a type A perfectionist firstborn raised by a type A perfectionist firstborn, after all. Lofty goals and proclamations are like my manna, but it's a dangerous line to walk between aiming high and missing out on the miracle that is right in front of us. Sometimes the bar needs to be lowered. Could I have more, do more, be more? Sure. Absolutely. But at what cost?

Because if it only ever was me here throwing thoughts onto a page and sharing them with you, and you sharing yours back with me, what an incredible and wonderful gift that would have been in the end.

And it's not just writing. It's everything.

Take my parenting. I mean, sure, I would love to be better—so much better—at motherhood. I wish I was more patient and played more and served more nutritious meals and had the resources and the energy to take us to interesting and educational places and lessons, and to get my daughter to stop wearing that one same too-small shirt every single day.

But if it was only ever this, if it was only ever me doing my mediocre half-ass best while serving up orange powder macaroni and wearing last night's pajamas and yesterday morning's makeup, wouldn't it still have been the most amazing thing I've ever done, hands down? Wouldn't it still have been full to bursting with incredible moments of breathtaking beauty? Wouldn't it still have been the truest love?

Or how about my marriage? Good God, there's an awful lot of room for improvement in my wifing skills. Just ask my husband. Like, I could stay awake past the kids' bedtime and spend some actual time hanging out with him, to start. Or we could plan outings together where we have idle time for conversation that isn't 100 percent about the children we just left and doesn't take place in stolen ten-second interludes in between emergencies. Except same, because if this was all we ever had, if it never went beyond raising these babies together and being lucky enough to have made a life with someone who loves the same people I love with the same irrational craziness I have, then wouldn't that have been more than enough? Wouldn't it have been the stuff of romance novels, the epilogue that happens after the drama dies down, the happily ever after?

Then there's my body. What if this was it? What if I never get skinny enough again to fit into the jeans I insist on holding onto even though they have just as much of a chance of being worn again as Oprah does of actually doing the "Thriller" dance with me at my book party? What if this is as perky as my boobs are going to be, or the smallest my waist is going to get, or the easiest waking up in the morning is going to be from here on out? Can that be enough? Or will it only ever be enough later, like it is now when I look back on pictures of myself when I was younger and think, "Oh, Liz. What an idiot you were to be wasting your time worrying about any of that nonsense when you had no idea how good you had it, you big fat dummy."

The thing about this truth is it works everywhere. My writing, my parenting, my marriage, my health, my career, my hair, my bank accounts, even my house. Sure, I'd love a cleaner and more modern everything, where the decor is more shabby chic and less "my kid smeared poop on the wall," but to look around at a place filled with the beautiful evidence of life and not see it as the gift it truly is would be as silly as looking around at a life filled with the same, and somehow coming up lacking. Because here's the real truth: If it was only ever this, only this and nothing more, then that would have been more than enough. It would, in fact, be everything. (Except Oprah. I still need her.)

Of course, there's one more thing to remember, and it might just be the biggest thing. We're not done. In what is both a heartbreaking and thrilling development, these babies will not always be babies. They will grow and change—and so will we—and life is nothing if not full of surprises. And maybe what the dream is, exactly, is less important than the fact that we have them at all to fall back on in the moments when the everyday minutiae of our beautiful lives feels a little too unbalanced. I wonder if this is what happened to my mother, if she just ran out of dreams and lost her will to keep going, and this maybe more than anything else is why I still try to cling to mine, however ridiculous they may seem. Because none of us could possibly know yet where our tightropes lead, but I for one am so excited to find out that I can barely remember to pull up my pants.

14

———◊———

A Letter to My Daughters

Dearest Girls,

Holy guacamole are you ever coming of age in an interesting time. Never have we as women been able to accomplish more. Together, we watched a woman run for president (and technically win), and I saw on your face for the first time that those words I tell you, all those times I said you can be anything you want, might actually be true.

And something big is definitely happening. Things are available to you that were not before. Glass ceilings are being shattered. Long-held prejudices that for years went unquestioned are being questioned, finally. Men who committed crimes against women are being called on it. A paradigm is starting to shift, albeit slowly.

Women are standing on the stage. And yet, we are still fighting the same old battles. We may be on the stage, but we are not necessarily accepted there. Not all the way, not yet.

I know that must be confusing for you. It's confusing for me too. So in a world where we are still offered a thousand false measures to stack our value against—our weight, the length of our hair, the size of our pores or our breasts or our pants, our likes and follows and number of views, our friends or lovers or degrees or bank accounts, how big our car is our how clean our house is or how fancy the title on our business card is, where we came from or where we are going or who we know—I wanted to make sure that you knew what I am only just now beginning to understand, which is this:

All the things in the world won't matter if you can't be alone with who you are, because in the end that's all there is, just that and nothing more.

Because here's the thing: the only true home you have is within yourself. And the foundation of that home may have been poured by Daddy and me, but the house was built by you. You have furnished it with your choices, you have hung your hopes and dreams on its walls and lit it up golden from within with the light of your spirit. We may visit—and I hope we do—but the only people who reside there always are you, sweet baby girls, and your God.

It is from that safe space that you will rise. It is from there that you will conquer. It is from there that you will change the world.

So what I ask of you is this. When doubt or fear or any of those false measures start to creep in, I need you to remember: I'm proud of you for what you have done already, and I'm proud of you for the things you have still yet to do, but here is the thing about being your mother: I'd love you just the same even if you never accomplished another thing. I love you no matter what. No. Matter. What.

And that's the kind of love I hope you can use. I hope you can take it back to the home in your heart and use it to reinforce the studs and seal up the leaks in the windows and patch the roof if it ever starts to let in any of that junk that doesn't belong. I hope it gives you a spark that can light the fire in your hearth and keep you warm long after you've drifted out of my embrace.

But mostly, I hope it's the kind of love you can learn to have for yourself, the unwavering, unflinching, untouchable kind that doesn't give a flying hoot about what your hair looks like or how many followers you have or how many little lines you have around your eyes when your face crinkles up in that smile you have that lights the sky right up.

It's the kind of love I wished I had for myself, and it's the only true thing I have to give to you. I am so hopelessly imperfect a mother, so novice and so new, but I can do this for you. Stand on my shoulders, Baby Girls, and climb right onto that stage. You belong there.

Love you forever,

Mom

15

———◊———

Sleepless Nights

It's three o'clock in the morning, our bedroom, any night, and I hear a noise. "Nick, did you hear that?" I ask my sleeping husband, hoping that the noise was just a remnant of the dream I was having about Brendan Fraser* and fried chicken because I would *really* like to go back to it.

Nick doesn't answer. The noise happens again, this time closer. Brendan is gone forever. "Nick!"

"What?!" Nick jumps up, immediately ready for action. It has always amazed me how he can do this, go from the deepest sleep directly into fight or flight. This is not a skill I have. There could be a crazed axe murderer standing in our bedroom and I would still contemplate whether I had enough of

———

*School Ties Brendan Fraser, for the love of God.

a window to press the snooze button one more time before he chopped me into little bits.

Nick is now staring at me, waiting. "There was a noise," I say, dragging myself up. "It's probably Luca. I'll move Gabby if you can go get him from his bed."

Gabby, of course, had fallen asleep in our bed hours before. She does this most nights because she shares a room with her sister and the two of them cannot be left alone together at bedtime or they will spend hours saying different variations of "butt" to each other and devolving into fits of giggles until sunrise. When I pick Gabby up to move her, she starts to murmur, still mostly asleep. "Purple elephant butt," I hear her say, and for punctuation she blows a long lazy raspberry into my shoulder.

"My thoughts exactly," I whisper back into her hair, which smells of shampoo and peanut butter. She's heavier than I remember, and when I bend to lift her, I can't do it. I have to instead gently nudge her into a state of semi-consciousness and walk her back to her bed. I'm just tired, I think, rationalizing, but then we'd gone to her annual physical and they'd shown me all plotted out nice on a chart how she is, beyond any ability for me to deny it, growing like a weed. I don't know why this surprises me, or why it makes my heart ache. I've been through this before, twice already, and will be through it at least once more before we're done. Children grow. It's a thing. I get it. Except I remember all those times over all those early years when I was carrying her here and there and everywhere and all the while always wanting to put her down so I could, just for a moment, hold something else: my dinner, my husband, my sanity. "Give me some *space*, for the love of God!" I'd yell, or pray, or mumble under my breath for the fourteenth time in a row like a crazy person, because I was, basically, a crazy person. Raising small children has that effect on people.

I tuck her into her own bed and turn off the fourteen lights around the house that her older sister and brother insist on leaving on every night. But then it's too dark, so I turn a couple back on. Just in case. When I get back to our room, Nick is already asleep (again, how does he do that?) and Luca is now in my spot. I move him over, which is fruitless because he moves right back. I squeeze into the ten-inch-wide strip of space left, turn onto my side, and pull the covers up. Luca pushes the covers back down and drapes a leg across my leg. At least it's warm.

Nick sighs next to me. "I thought you were asleep," I say.

"I was faking, mostly."

I'm quiet for a second, not pretending to sleep (who does that?) but thinking about how I will never fall back asleep now and wondering if we have any fried chicken in the fridge. I look over and across Luca, who is laying sideways now like a wall between Nick and me. Nick seems so very far away. "Do you think the thrill is gone?" I ask him, only half kidding. He snorts.

I wonder about this a lot, and I don't mean fried chicken, although yes, that too. This marriage with children thing looks so different than what it looked like *before* babies, and I wonder sometimes if that's a natural evolution or more of a devolution. Where before we were unequivocally together, just Nick and I and our life and our dreams and our very small grocery bill that I took completely for granted, now we are the bookends to this large family. I wonder, have we expanded as a unit to make space for these kids, or have we inevitably had to drift apart in order to fit it all in, the way we have in this bed? I don't know the answer. What I do know is sometimes I miss Nick, all the way over there. I miss him the way you miss something you used to have and totally took for granted, like collagen or personal space or uninterrupted sleep, or the way I now miss my mother.

Nick and I went to a wedding recently, and of course I got weepy. I always do; I can't help it. I've cried at every wedding I've ever been to but also any wedding I see on TV, including cartoon weddings and weddings in commercials. There's something just so beautiful to me about that unbridled optimism that only love and big beginnings and an open bar can create. At this wedding, like at all weddings, everyone did that glass-clinking thing that people do to make the bride and groom kiss, only the bride must have not known about the glass-clinking thing because she held her glass up in cheers and took a big gulp from it instead of kissing, like it was a big drinking game and we all just wanted to get her a little buzzed up. I fell in love with her a little then, or maybe it was before then, when they stood in front of each other all doe-eyed and fresh-faced, reciting their vows on the precipice of all of the things that come after.

And maybe it wasn't love but jealousy, that old-married-people-at-a-wedding thing that is half "Oh, lord, just wait until they find out" and half "I would give a kidney to be back there again, still." Because sure, I miss it, how could I not? I miss how when we first started dating Nick had this way of looking at me like I was something delicate and fragile that needed to be handled with care, and it was the first time I had ever seen myself as anything other than hard edged and mostly broken. I miss the way we could sit across a table in a dimly lit restaurant and talk for hours about everything and nothing at all and it would feel like time had stopped and the universe had shrunk down to just us two and a candle and a bottle of cheap wine. I miss being able to banter back and forth about how we wanted to spend the time that spread out before us languid and easy and open, so arrogant, like it would always be that way and we could make it into whatever we wanted.

And today? Well today, he looks at our children the way he used to look at me. Today we lie across a big bed, a child or two tangled in between us, and it's like the universe has expanded just enough to fit the whole six of us nice and snug. Today we don't plan and plot and worry as much about the future, not because it's not still laid out there—it is, I hope—but because what's there in front of us right now is so big and so needy that it's hard to find the space to dream. And that's what this all is, really, when it comes down to it. It's a question of space. There's only so much space, in our hearts, in our lives, in our days, in our beds. And in what little is left for me I lay, snuggling Luca for as long as I can tolerate until I concede that I can't exactly breathe and have to push him over a little towards his father's side. Nick promptly pushes him back. It's a space negotiation, a dance we know so well we can do it in our sleep, although usually for me sleep is elusive from this point on.

The truth is we haven't had a good night's sleep in years. With four kids total and all of them still relatively young enough to still wake up in the middle of the night sick or scared or wet or thirsty or just alone, it's a nightly event that at least one and sometimes more pads into our room at some point, holding a blanket or a stuffed something that has seen better days. I'll roll over and look at the clock, and inevitably there's a moment where my stomach sinks at the mental math of how much more sleep I just might get if I am lucky, but still, I always try to make them some space. It's one of my rules. We make space.

I know it's a controversial subject, and I know (and respect) that it's not for everyone. I know the parenting magazines would probably frown on it. Perhaps more importantly—to me—I know the lack of sleep has likely taken years off my life or, at the very least, made me look like it has. And yes, I've read the sleep-training books and talked to the doctors and let myself fantasize about what it would be like to just once sleep wholly and deeply through the night, and let me tell you, the prospect is absolutely lovely. But I feel like this is something I need to do, and for me there is a good reason. It's this.

When I was sixteen and stopped eating and the anxiety problem that had been a manageable hum in the background of my childhood before became a loud and constant scream that I couldn't ignore, nighttime was always the worst time. I would toss and turn for hours, trying to convince myself I wasn't hungry, sick, and falling quickly into a hole that was too big for me to pull myself out of alone.

My mother and I were not in the best place then either—not necessarily because of her addiction, not that I knew of anyway—but more because I was growing up and the space between the two of was growing wider, too. But even across that expanse, I knew she saw what was happening to me and worried, even if she didn't understand or know how to help. One night when it all got to be too much, I did something out of desperation that I hadn't done since I was maybe six and scared of thunder: I crept into her room and climbed into her bed. She didn't say anything, not that I remember, and I assumed she was asleep. But I pulled the covers up and settled my head on her pillow and closed my eyes and then I felt it, so light I thought I imagined it at first, her hand resting on my back. I'm sure it was the first time we had touched like that in months, maybe years. Sometimes I think maybe that hand saved my life. Or maybe it was just the bridge across the space between us that got me through the night into the next day, which eventually got me into recovery. At the very least, I know this: I fell instantly asleep.

For a short while then it became a routine of sorts, one that we never spoke about in the daylight. I don't know if she appreciated those small moments of togetherness we had there like I did or if she just tolerated them because she knew I was sick, and she's gone now so I can't ask. I know she struggled to sleep herself, and that a consistent interruption every night was probably not helping her much in the long run, but never once did she complain or tell me to go away, not then, not in the deepest dark of night. She made me space, without even understanding what a gift she was giving me. And I will do the same for my babies for as long as I can. It's the least I can do.

You see, most days I'm not a great mother, not like the ones you see on TV or read about in parenting magazines that say my babies should learn to self-soothe. My temper is shorter than I'd like, and I yell more than anyone should ever admit to. I am terrible at braiding hair or remembering to sign the thousands of papers that come home every day stuffed into four different backpacks. I'm much too distracted and I'm tired and I make so many mistakes daily that usually I lose count before lunchtime.

But at night? This is still something I can do, what my own mother did for me all of those years ago. I can make space. I can let them in, rest my hand lightly on their backs, feeling their soft breath as they settle next to me and—if only just for that moment—help them rest easier in the knowledge that they don't have to be alone. I know it's not forever and their need, huge now with little-kid troubles, like night terrors and bed-wetting and things under the bed, will evolve into bigger-kid needs that are harder to satisfy, and likely then into the not needing at all. It's a prospect that both gets me through my tired days and guts me. But for now I know this: for as long as I can, I will help them sleep, even if it means that some nights I don't.

So this is what it looks like these days, Nick and I tag-teaming our way through the nights, passing kids to each other through the space we've made like relay batons. And it feels like a master dance that took years to choreograph and yet still is so tenuous that one string pulled could unravel it into a pile of children at our feet. I remember my question, the half joke. *Is* the thrill gone? Or is the truth that yes, there is space between us now that wasn't there before we had kids, but it is there because we have done this intentionally, come apart so that we could make the space that they needed? I mean, when you think about it like that, it's actually kind of lovely.

Sure, I miss who we were back then the same way I miss my youth, or my pre-baby body, or who I was in high school. Fondly, or nostalgically, even. This life we have now is hard. Marriage is hard and raising children is hard and when we are struggling, with the daily minutiae or the big, ugly things, like loss and grief and pain and the very deep darkness of night, what is more thrilling than knowing that someone is close by?

And isn't that what we pledge to each other, in all those wedding vows that I weep along to or when we first hold our babies or however we cement the bonds of family? None of this is ever going to be perfect, and often it's going to be a bit of a shit storm, but I'll be damned if any of us tries to weather it alone. That's what family is, blood or chosen. It's people to walk through the storm with you. Or sleep through it, a hand resting lightly on your back just so you know they're there. It's the making of space.

Everything else is just a season, always changing. This is the sleepless season, the season of little feet on my neck, the season of being needed in the middle of the night. And our wedding season is over now, which is too bad, because after Nick fell asleep for real and Luca finally settled, I laid awake picturing it: me in the perfect off-white, forgiving around the waistline, stain-resistant dress, gazing lovingly into Nick's eyes and answering the priest's question, "Do you, Liz, agree to muddle through the shit storm with this man?" with a resounding "Yes. I do."

The crowd erupts into cheers, clinking their glasses with gleeful abandon. I raise my glass, to them, to Nick, to my mama, and to all four of our babies. And I take a big drink, thrilled.

16

————◊————

The Boy on the Couch

"Your face!" I said to Jack one night not too long ago, reaching over, touching his cheek. There was a fresh scratch—nothing major—running from his temple to his eye, ugly and red.

He moved away from my hand, not even looking up from the TV. "It's nothing. I scraped it playing baseball earlier. It's fine. Don't make it a thing."

I was stung. Don't make it a thing? This child, now basically a teenager, had come to me for years, every single thing "a thing": every bump, scratch, scare, and emission presented to me to patch or soothe or clean. His entire existence was a thing. I don't know when that changes, really, but I can tell you it does change, so slowly that I don't think we realize it's even happening until it has happened already, and we're sitting there next to a man-child and realize we haven't had to patch a wound or wipe a tear in longer than we can remember.

Of course Jack's the first of our brood, so there's others coming up behind him still and my days of kissing boo-boos aren't behind me, not yet, thank God. I gave Luca (who for now is still unequivocally a child) his bath the other night and for a while I just watched him play in the hip-high water, willing time—or maybe myself—to slow so I could do what they've all warned me to do, all those well-meaning strangers who say to appreciate every moment. But all that did was make me tense and breathy and when I couldn't sit any longer, I washed his hair with the baby shampoo that smells like optimism, his curls straightened out and stretched longer down his back than they ever had, and I had that thought, the nervous anthem of motherhood: it's going so fast.

And it has gone fast. It still all feels like a whirlwind when I look back on it, how babies had been carried and born, one after another, until there were four and the house was one big hurricane dumpster fire of Cheerios, poop, and breast milk, and my body had stretched itself into bizarre and unrecognizable shapes and not quite exactly bounced back, and maybe the same could be said for my marriage, and yet I sat there, fourth perfect little one soaking, the best one yet, and I could imagine a fifth.

Sure I could.

Hell, I could imagine a sixth and maybe then a set of twins, and on and on until we had a little army of deranged miniature versions of our weirdest selves, running (never walking) on the hardwoods back and forth until the noise, deafening at first, became so regular that we didn't hear it anymore. Nick had always made fun of me for wanting so many, suggesting probably only half-jokingly that I could only put off the inevitability of them all growing up and leaving me for so long, no matter how many there were.

I definitely thought there would be more, too, thought there was no way I'd ever feel done, until the feeling *done* started to creep in. And of course it wasn't all at once; nothing real ever is. It was moments, little flashes, some so quick I missed them and others I glimpsed only after they had passed, the way you will notice a blue jay in the window above the sink while you're washing your four thousandth baby bottle of the day and your eyes have started to cross a little with the repetitive gorgeous exhaustion of it all.

"What was that I just felt?" I would ask myself. It was a feeling I knew, a deep haunting sense of nostalgia, really, the kind of blinding weepy sentimentality we can churn up in our hearts if we think too long and hard about how innocent we were when we were little and still believed in magic and Santa Claus and our mothers, or if we accidentally catch a glimpse of ourselves naked in the full-length mirror after we get out of the shower and we remember how we used to be so perfect and unmarred when we were teenagers and wasted it all hating ourselves anyway. It was the kind of nostalgia you feel for something that has passed, a season that has ended, falling just like a gentle mist and settling first onto the ends of my eyelashes and shoulders and then deeper.

And I knew with Luca. I knew in that ache the way we all do, that this was the last time. That sometime soon, even as I walked through the same long days and sleepless nights I'd worn a rut across for a decade, I'd give my last bath, or change my last diaper, or roll over half awake in the wee hours of dawn and press a baby to my breast for the last time. I looked hard at

Luca there playing in the water, willed myself to remember this moment through the exhaustion and the postpartum depression and the wild grief of having lost my mother just weeks before he was born, but I also wonder if it was even possible, or if the true appreciation and gratitude for what we have had can only come with the deep longing of hindsight.

If I let the edges blur for a second, it could be a decade or so before, me still bathing his brother Jack in the kitchen sink of our first house the way I did most nights after dinner, after the pots and pans had been rinsed and dried. Even though I was so incredibly tired all of the time those days, and even though my feet ached just standing there on the cold hardwoods, I'd always looked forward to those baths, the last few minutes together before the long night stretched ahead. There was that moment after he was wrapped in a towel and smelled like that same shampoo when his own wet curls would stick to the soft place at the back of his neck and his absurdly long eyelashes would clump together and brush against his cheeks as his eyes drifted towards closing. And for those few minutes every night of that first year of parenthood, I'd hold my first baby and think maybe I *can* do this.

And then I would put him to bed and he would scream, and the tension would sweep back into my shoulders like a hot wave and I knew nope, I was wrong, tricked by the stupid optimistic-smelling shampoo again. I couldn't possibly do this; there was no way. And Nick and I would lock eyes at the sound of that first cry, half allies in this war and half enemies, each of us hoping the other would be the one to get up. Eventually someone would, and the other one would a little while after that, and it went on like that for nights into weeks into years, and all of a sudden all of this had gone by in the blink of an eye and it was this new little one in the bathtub, and I had done it, or at least was doing it, with four babies all alive and mostly well so far, and sometimes, for a few minutes after the bath anyway, even relatively clean.

It's still so hard so much of the time, but I'm not sure it is ever as hard as it was then, that first year. In that uncertain and terrifying beginning, I used to lay in bed next to baby Jack, his body pressed against mine after he had fallen asleep nursing, his mouth still moving even after the breast had fallen away, and wonder if I held him tightly enough if our heartbeats would synchronize. I had read somewhere in one of my thousands of baby books that newborn babies and their mamas will regulate each other's body temperatures, and so I thought maybe the same could happen with our hearts: his tiny, perfect, unmarred-by-life-or-loss-bird-heart that I had listened to on a Doppler ultrasound months before I met him, slowing to meet mine or the reverse: mine—a little rusty and visibly cracked in a few places—speeding up, pumping this new blood of motherhood into my veins.

I had all these things I wanted to tell him then, in those first days and weeks: about how I had no idea (just none at all) what love was until I met him, and how he was the most incredible thing I had ever seen, even if he did have a little dusting of black fur covering a lot of his body. I wanted to make all of the promises to him: that I would protect him, and that it would be beautiful, and that nothing would hurt. But he was sleeping—thank you, sweet Jesus—and only a fool would wake their baby, even if it's with whispered promises. So instead I would just press my hand into the fleshy part of his belly, feel the slight give of his still-soft ribs, and pull him closer to me.

My mother brought dinner over one night in those early days, and after eating in shifts so one of us could hold the baby, she'd looked down at Jack, finally, amazingly, sleeping in her arms, and said, her voice sad and serious so I knew it was important, "If we could just know when we were adults the kind of love that had welcomed us into the world, I don't think we would be lonely ever again." I think of those words now as my firstborn sits close to me on the couch, a fully formed human, and asks me not to make it a thing. When she said it, I'd assumed she was talking about the baby in her arms, about Jack, but now I wondered if she meant this instead. Maybe she was talking about this loneliness, the loneliness that sits on the other side of having tried to raise your babies the way we're supposed to, so that they are able and willing to go out on their own and make a life that doesn't depend on us anymore. I bend my head to him like I have been doing for a decade, inhale deeply, and search for a trace of that sweet baby smell. He grew so much this year—an inch per month—that I had wondered more than once if I watched him sleep, could I see it happening? Or was it imperceptible, creeping up slowly the way the years themselves have?

When I was young, five maybe, my family rented a cabin on a lake for a week in the summer. One evening my sister and I went out on the dock after dinner to feed the fish pieces of our Popsicles while our parents washed dishes and watched us out the window. We sat on the edge, dangling our feet and letting them come close to the surface of the water, but never touching, because one time my toe had been mistaken by an overly eager fish for a chunk of bread, and trust me when I say that's a mistake that happens only once. The dock was wet just a little and

Katherine was wearing a bathing suit, and even as I watched the fish chase the Popsicle chunks and the shadows of my toes, I thought I could see her in the edge of my periphery, sliding ever so slightly closer to the edge. But then I would turn, look at her straight on, and she wasn't moving at all, but was still there next to me, Popsicle in hand.

Except then suddenly she wasn't. She was in the water, or more accurately, under it. I remember no splash or fall, just her there and then not there, and then under the surface of the water, her totally calm face turned up, eyes wide open, looking at me. She had to have been not much more than two years old then, certainly didn't know how to swim, and neither did I, but I called for my parents and my dad came running down the dock in what felt like two amazingly long strides. He jumped in fully clothed to save her, and that splash I do remember: it was spectacular.

Back on the couch with this boy, I think of my sister and how when I looked at her full-on she was solid, unmoving, just my little sister on the dock with a green Popsicle. This boy is like that, just a boy on my couch watching TV. My boy. But when I turn away, to dinner or his siblings or my own life, I swear I see him slipping in my periphery, just a little at a time, towards the edge. I know too that one day, I am going to look up and he won't be next to me anymore. There won't be a splash or with this one, not even a jump, just a quiet edging towards his own life he is making out there in the world, away from where he started, pressed up against my chest. The biggest changes happen this way, I'm sure of it now. A thousand micro movements until all of the sudden, what was there isn't anymore, the way my sister was on the docks and then wasn't, the way later my mother was in our lives and then wasn't, the way eventually each one of these babies, once a literal part of me, will be gone.

And I am proud and grateful and humbled by this miracle of witnessing, the gift of having sat on the figurative dock with Jack (or the other three, who are each no less miraculous; it's just that he is the first) and watching them prepare to launch. But I am also worried about what will happen to my heart, since it has indeed regulated itself to the heartbeats of the four small humans in this house, and I'm not sure it even knows how to beat on its own again. I believe this is the loneliness my mother tried to warn me about, how our hearts will have swollen to make room for the babies the same way our bodies once did, and when their constant need for us has faded away, the open space in our hearts will sag a little to match our bellies and our breasts, never exactly being able to feel as full again. All those warnings to cherish every moment never made any sense to me until the moments had gone by.

Except maybe she wasn't right, at least not all of the way. Because it's not a zero-sum game, this life. These children will grow and probably leave, eventually, just as my mother grew away from me and left herself, but what's also true is that when things are lost, we are not left empty. We are left with the gift of all those years, all those memories, and all the ways having lived through it has changed us into better versions of ourselves. So while I can barely remember either of them anymore the way they were, not the sleeping baby my mother held or my mother, I can remember bits and pieces: the way Jack would wrinkle his top lip before he started to cry, or how the black furry hair he was covered in faded soon and left behind the softest skin I'd ever felt in my life. I can remember my mother's laugh, her hands, the furrow she would get in-between her eyebrows when she was disappointed in me. And the gift is this: I can look back and remember a boy in the sink and smell the soap, and yet it's hard for me to recall how terrified we were walking through those first days. I can remember my mother there in my kitchen, rocking my sleeping baby, and I don't have to tie that memory to the pain of all the times she wasn't there later on. We can give ourselves the grace of nostalgia, even if you couldn't pay us enough to go back to living the years we are nostalgic for again. And as that first baby slips ever more away into his life, I find myself slipping too, into that grace.

But then I look head-on again and he's not gone yet; he's next to me on the couch and he has this scratch—nothing major—that runs from his temple to his eye. It has started to bleed just a tiny bit, and it's lined in garnet dots, a delicate red bracelet like the one his father gave me for Christmas when I was so swollen with this baby inside me, and I'd woken up to realize I had my very first hemorrhoid (Herman), and I was completely afraid that my body was turning itself inside out. "I will not make this a thing," I tell myself, but I'm afraid if I look away, Jack will slide fully away. So I sit and stare at the scratch, will my hand to stay in my lap, not reach over, not brush his cheek, but I can't help it. I press my finger to the scratch, pull back little tiny beads of blood on my fingertip. It's a marvel, his blood, how it is there when it once wasn't.

And he slides then, because I looked away, down at my finger. It's a tiny thing, nothing you would even notice if you weren't sitting right there. He doesn't even look away from the TV. All he does is shift, then lean, then exhale, but this slide, amazingly, is different. This time he somehow ends up closer to me on the couch. I will not make this a thing either, I tell myself, even as I do make it a thing in my own little heart, which is synchronizing itself right up like when I plug in the drained iPad. I still want to make those promises: tell him it's going to be beautiful out there and nothing is going to hurt, but I can feel next to me now that his ribs are solid and he needs the promises less. I also still know deep down that one day I am going to look up and he won't be next to me anymore. Just maybe not today.

17

———◊———

Better Than We Ever
Were Before

Luca got hurt one evening when he was three or so. It wasn't anything serious, not in the grand scheme of things, but something accidental, like a door flung open in playful exuberance by his older sister with his small foot underneath that resulted in a banged-up toe. So not that scary kind of serious, anyway, and that's not the point, not what I want to tell you.

What I want to tell you is the rest of it. How he came to Nick and me, crying. The two of us were sitting at the dinner table, lost in that holy moment between when the kids have finished eating and left the table and when we have to force ourselves to begin the long process of cleaning it all up. Luca was crying, but this was nothing new. The four of them together are a constant cacophony of shrieks, some in pain, some in pleasure; it's often hard to tell. We were only half paying attention anyway. It's not often we're left alone to talk, just husband and wife. This time is sacred. It's church.

Nick was closer to him, my view blocked partially by the table and the dirty dishes piled high, so he realized first. "Liz?" he said, and from his voice instantly I knew too. This one was for real. "Maybe you should look at this?" And just like that we were in motion, all six of us swooping into action like a trauma team. I had Luca in my arms before I knew I was up, Nick clearing space for him by the sink so we could wash the wound out. The other kids scattered to four corners of the house and raced back breathless with their offerings: BAND-AIDs, blankies, well-worn stuffed lovies, a sippy cup full of warm milk. We were perfect in that moment, everyone assuming their role, no arguing or hitting or jockeying for position. If only just for a second, all the members of this family were united. We had come together.

It was only many hours and one urgent care visit later, when the boy was bandaged up and then put down asleep in my bed, that we came back undone, everyone shrieking again and each for their own reason: Jack didn't want to be separated from his video games. Maria didn't want to be separated from me. Gabby, made especially vulnerable by the hours she'd spent blaming herself for Luca's injury in a downward spiral of self-blame and self-loathing, was reduced to a kicking pile on the floor when I committed the atrocity of removing her socks. (It was hot. They were dirty.) Nick and I were edgy, tired, and I'd been wearing a bra and real pants for much longer into the night than I'm accustomed to.

If someone was watching us from the outside, I imagine we would have looked like glass cracking under the pressure of water: first the splintering, a thousand tiny fissures, and then finally the giving way, the release, the letting go of any pretense of trying to hold anything together.

A few days ago, a reader wrote to ask me a question. She too had lived through a suffering, one bigger than a torn-up toe, I'd imagine, but the truth is the bigness or smallness of the suffering isn't even important to anyone but her, and anyway that's not what I want to tell you, either. What I want to tell you is the universal part, the rest of it, how she had borne the weight of the suffering, stayed strong through the onslaught, and survived. She had been a warrior. And then the immediate suffering had passed, her life was quiet again and she tried to settle back into it, grateful. Except she couldn't. "I was okay," she wrote to me, "through all of it. I was okay. And now I'm not. Why would I feel worse now that it's all over?"

I read her words and remembered coming home once from a funeral with my mother when I was a teenager. A woman we knew, a mother of children I went to school with, had taken her own life. For reasons still unclear to me, my mother had spoken at the funeral, and I don't remember what she said exactly but I remember watching her approach the altar, the sound of her heels clicking into the sad silence of the cavernous church, and trying to imagine what it must have felt like to be those now-motherless kids seated near her. How were they still upright, I wondered. How were they still drawing breath? I asked my mother as much when we drove home together.

"It's not now when the falling apart happens," she'd said. "It's later. It's when this is all over, when the casseroles have been eaten and the long-distance family has traveled back home. It's then, in the quiet, when it's safe. That's when we break."

It didn't make a lot of sense to me then, but it does now. Of course it's after the suffering that we fall apart. What good would a warrior be in battle who breaks at first sight of a weapon? How would those motherless kids have survived if they didn't shield themselves in protective armor and forge through those first few days, swinging and cutting and trudging until the deluge ended and the clouds parted? How would the six of us have been any help to a broken and bloodied Luca the night he'd hurt himself if we each had not steeled ourselves against his suffering? How would my dear reader have lived to come out on the other side, ready to heal?

And I remembered sitting on the couch one night shortly after my own mother had died. Luca was only a few days old then, and he had fallen asleep on me while nursing, still halfway latched on. I thought I'd been strong through the weeks after my mother's death, strong enough to birth my baby, strong enough—I hoped—to take care of him and myself and my family while we adjusted to life as six. But Nick had been watching me through all of this, I could feel it; I heard the way he talked to me then as if I was fragile, as if he was afraid he would say the wrong thing and I would break. When Luca had nodded off, Nick brought me a glass of wine that I sipped, trying to let myself remember how simple pleasures like the bite of a good red or the stillness of the house at night could ease the exhaustion off my back, if only for a moment. It wasn't working.

I can see now how Nick was right, how I was brittle then with sleeplessness and my own grief-madness sitting so heavy on me it was palpable, a black and ugly mass swirling threateningly over everything I did. But if you had asked me then how I was doing, I would have laughed too shrilly or smiled a little too eagerly and insisted I was okay, really, getting along just fine, thanks for asking, now please go away. And I'd convinced myself of the same, carrying on with folding the laundry and making the coffee and waking every hour to nurse and every morning to get three kids off to school because I had to, somebody did. But I could taste the metal of insanity in my mouth and feel the buzz of exhaustion in my bones. I'm convinced now that the early days of grief are spent tiptoeing a little numb around the edge of a hole so deep and dark you can't see the bottom, all while knowing sooner or later you are going to drop in and shatter.

Luca stirred then in my lap and I held my breath and willed him not to wake. The house creaked. The baby settled. I held the wine glass in my hand, now empty, and eventually even the weight of that was too much, and I threw it against the wall. I don't remember why. I don't remember who cleaned it up, or if the sound of glass shattering woke the baby, but I do remember then thinking how jealous I was of the glass's ability to just burst into a thousand pieces with no pretense required of having to hold it together. And this is when the breaking happens, because it has to. It happens when the alternative—continuing to hold it together—is more painful than letting ourselves fall apart.

———◊———

A couple years later I took my family to the Cape on vacation, a hop, skip, and a jump from where we used to go with my mother when I was young. I meant to bring her ashes with me, which I have sitting in the linen cabinet upstairs next to the bathroom cleaner and the extra set of sheets, but in the chaos of packing, I forgot them. I'd planned to scatter them into the sea, and still do, but this marked the third year in a row that I'd been ocean-bound since she died and had forgotten to bring them along.

"I forgot my mother," I texted Nick from the rest stop. We make the seven-plus hour drive in separate cars because we want to stay married. "Again."

"Maybe it's not time yet," he said back.

Maybe it's not. Maybe there's still work to do before I can let go. My mother and I were in active battle for a long time. We battled with each other, sure, but we also battled separately against our own selves. It took a long time to shed the armor. It took a long time to allow myself to break the way I knew I needed to and by the time I did, she was right, everyone had long since gone home. The casseroles were gone. I was alone, which maybe was good, because for a while I was like shattered glass, this jagged, ugly thing, something that needed to be handled with extra care lest it draw blood. And it took an even longer time to put the pieces back together into some configuration that made sense in this new world, this world where my mother wasn't here and I had to try to not let that realization keep washing over me and knocking me down. But time passes, even when it seems like it won't, even when you can't imagine ever being anything other than sharp. The waves of a regular-person life will patiently lap at your edges, gently turning you over and around until you find what was once sharp can wear smooth.

Once we made it to the sea, the kids and I walked the beach, them looking for seashells and me looking for some peace. They filled their pockets and pails to the point of bursting, but only once did something catch my eye enough for me to bend and pluck it from the wet sand. It was a small piece of sea glass, pretty in the sun and worn smooth from the water, the same shade of blue my mother's eyes had been, the same color Luca's eyes are now. I let it roll in my fingers and remembered the sharp shards of glass from the shattered wine glass years before. This is the progression, I'm pretty sure. I'm not sharp anymore; I won't draw blood. But I also will never be the whole person I was before. Yet I can be someone new entirely, maybe someone pretty still, someone smoothed over by the waves of time that still glitters when the sun hits just right.

It was quiet on the beach that day. There were some families, a few hardcore children like mine who can stomach the freezing cold water, a few paunch-bellied men with enviable tans and expensive metal detectors, a young couple here or there driven to distraction by each other's exposed skin. And then there were the women, like there always are, at least since I started paying attention.

They're every couple hundred feet or so on the decent days, dotting the length of the beachside and intentionally set apart from whatever sparse crowds there were. They're older—my mother's age or what she would have been had she lived—or past it, their faces and their bodies soft and lined with the stories of what they have seen and survived. Usually they have books open in their laps but mostly don't glance at them, pulled in by the majestic blue show of the waves where they sit, toes in the sand. Sometimes they smile at me as I pass, and sometimes I try not to look at them because to do so feels a little like an invasion, like I'm breaking the spell of the moment and drawing them back earth-side. And there's this too, which I haven't told anyone: from a distance and with the sand in my eyes, sometimes I let myself pretend one of them is my mom. It's where she would want to be, that much I know for sure, and it's what I would hope she would get on the other side, that peace, that beauty, that majesty. That chance to rest in solitude after a lifetime of mothering and serving and, also, suffering.

Oftentimes when I was finally and gloriously breaking apart in the aftermath of her death, I would let myself fret over what heaven looked like. It kept me up at night, the worrying that she wouldn't fit in or they'd have the wrong kind of toilet paper or not enough of the low-sodium Triscuits she liked so much. She'd called me from rehab a couple times and complained about all of that junk: the food, the people, the way not sleeping in your own bed at night can wear away at a person until they lose the ability to make the appropriate small talk and shrink away into the corner, unnoticed. It took a while of walking past them but eventually, when I was ready, I saw these women on the beach and I saw their peace and I knew. My mother would have wanted to spend her days sitting low in a beach chair, a good book untouched at her side, watching the waves wash the pain of her past away. It's part of why I stopped trying to make eye contact with the women, to be honest. Because if I looked up and it was her and she saw me, I knew it would break the spell. I'd rather see her fuzzy in my periphery as my kids splash each other, hoping their laughter carries on the ocean breeze down to where she is, listening, watching, healing, hoping too she knew we were there, in the same space, even if just for a little while. For now.

———◊———

In the morning after our urgent care visit, I went into Luca's bedroom to wake him. He turned towards me, awake, and I asked him how his foot felt. "Does it hurt?" I said, leaning over him where he was still wrapped up, snuggled in the bed.

He closed his eyes, and for a second I thought he had drifted back to sleep. But then they fluttered open again, a hint of sweet smile in them. He stretched his foot out, and wiggled his toes. "I think maybe it's better now," he said, "than it ever was before." And damn if that wasn't the truth for me too.

Because—and this is the piece my mother forgot to tell me, the other half of the equation—if it's in the quiet where we fall apart, it's also in the falling apart that we can finally start to heal. Armor, while often the only thing keeping us alive during the onslaught, is not a soothing balm to an open wound once the battle is over. But as anyone who has ever taken off a bra at the end of a long day knows, the removal of the armor *is*. The reader who had reached out to me wasn't doing anything wrong; she was doing what we all have to do to stay alive. And we are capable of such amazing feats of strength, all of us are. I believe this deeply in my heart. I've watched people shoulder the most amazing burdens and climb out of the deepest holes, often while carrying their families in their arms. Even my mother, as sick as she was, pushed through it enough to raise two babies herself, and we—my sister and me—are still here, still falling apart and putting ourselves back together, still trying to make our way along the path and learn the lessons and heal, and maybe, if we can, carry her memory with us along the way.

So while I don't know if I will ever be able to fully let her go, I don't know either if I need to. I don't know if those ashes will make it seaside or if they will stay in that cabinet next to the other makings of a normal life. Maybe, if we're going to be honest, I will never be able to let go because I don't really want to, and someday my own kids will be cleaning out my house after I too am gone, and they'll find a dusty Ziploc bag next to the plunger and wonder what I—the woman who throws everything out—could ever have held onto for so long. But I can tell you this: nestled inside that Ziploc bag now is the prettiest piece of sea glass I've ever seen. I brought it home so I could remember that this, all of it—the cuts and the scrapes and the losses and the pain—is an evolution. We survive and then we shatter and then we heal, and if we're lucky, we are better for having been through it.

As for my mother and me, the road to healing is long and convoluted, and I'm not sure we were even headed in the right direction when she died, but I know that we haven't stopped traveling on it just because she's not here anymore. And in some respects the way we've come back together after her death, after the biggest shattering apart there is, is better than the way we kept trying to fit together (and failing) while she was still here. And I am a better version of myself, a better mother, a better woman, and a better daughter too, for having let myself crack open enough to let the light of faith shine in.

Epilogue

Dog Person

I was never a dog person; nope, not me. Growing up we had cats here and there, and I assumed a dog was a bigger, smellier version of a cat without the dignity needed to poop in a litter box. "Why bother with that mess," I'd think all smug, watching all of the dog people in my neighborhood walk up and down the street, holding plastic baggies filled with vileness, letting them swing precariously back and forth like they were the latest Coach wristlet.

And then, a decade ago, we were robbed. It was mild as home invasions go, which is the absurd kind of thing you learn to say after a lifetime of urban living. Either way, we weren't home at the time, and all they made away with was an old clunky laptop and a large beer growler we had repurposed into a jar to collect spare change. Oh, they'd looked for more, throwing my collection of hoochie hoops I'd bought at Claire's around my bedroom in disgust, but we didn't have much. A life pro tip for people looking to rob houses: stay away from the ones with kids. We can't afford anything nice, and even if we could, the kids would suck all the value out of it.

Its relative mildness aside, the break-in left me unnerved, which is a polite way of saying I had a full-on nervous breakdown: crying, wailing, writing passive aggressive messages to the robbers in my kids' chalk on the driveway. Eventually, I caught my breath, clear-headed with purpose. I knew what we needed to do.

"We need a dog," I said. "For protection."

"No way," Nick said.

So the next day my sister and I followed a newspaper ad out to a farm, and a man put a puppy into my arms, and before Nick could finish saying, "Over my dead body," we were home and the dog was named Boss, as in Springsteen. He was sweet and crazy and bite-y and bark-y and did not, despite my best intentions, have any interest in using the litter box.

I'd say it happened all at once, this not-a-dog-person becoming one, except it wasn't like that. It's a slow creep, so slow you don't realize it until it's too late, until you're out there scooping up poop and carrying it around in a little bag like it's cute and you don't even know who you are anymore. Eventually, I was talking to him too, and not just commands or directions, but asking questions, like what should we make for dinner tonight or who was going to win in the midterms or would he like his belly scratched, would he, would he, who's a good boy, who's a good boy, who's a good boy. Barf. It's amazing how I didn't realize I'd lost myself, still fancying myself not so much of a dog person as I took him in the shower with me once after a flea medicine mishap, using up half a bottle of the good shampoo and letting him take the good towel while I drip-dried, shivering.

I tell you all this, of course, because we lost him. It was like before, a slow creep into sickness that happened so quietly no one noticed until it was undeniable, ugly, scary, and in our faces. I cried the whole time, from start to finish, and I'm crying now as I tell you this story, which is funny because when I lost my mother it took me time and a whole lot of processing to finally break down, and even then there were all these stages of emotion I had to get through before I found my grief: anger, shame, betrayal, flat-out denial. I miss my mother like crazy, but our relationship was complicated. Relationships with people often are.

But dogs? This is as simple as it gets.

And I say this to you, but I don't have to. You already know. To have had a dog is to have known what it is to be simply and completely loved, no matter what, even when you don't deserve it. It is to have been knitted together with a string so fine and delicate that you didn't even see it wrapped around you, woven through the everyday, the mundane and the routine, the chaos and the tragedy, the lazy and the intimate. So it stands to reason, I suppose, that to lose a dog—to unravel—is maybe the purest grief I have ever felt.

A few weeks before Boss died, on a whim that both my husband and my sister would tell me was really super weird, I bought a bottle of the perfume my mother had worn her whole life, and I started wearing it. "But why," Nick asked me, genuinely worried. "Why would you want to smell like your mother?"

I had no answer, not then, not yet. But then the night before he died, I laid down on the floor next to Boss, put myself right up by his face, felt his labored exhales fall on my chest. "If you need to go," I told him, quiet, "you can."

He softened.

"Look for my mother up there," I said. "She'll take care of you. Give her the sloppiest doggy kiss ever, and trust me when I say she's only pretending to be annoyed. She just doesn't know she's a dog person yet."

I meant it too; no one knows more than me that people can change, and I don't think that applies only when we are walking this side of life. It's an evolution, after all, this business of learning how to love and how to let go. It is the dance of this life, the most precious gift there is and the hardest thing to do, especially when we're sleep deprived, lonely, and afraid. I'm not trying to pretend I have the moves down or that there's any element of grace in me at all while I fumble along, but in the end, I don't think that's what matters. What matters is that we keep going, in spite of the pain. No, through the pain. Because the other side can be quite beautiful, from what I've seen.

So I got up off of the floor where I had been crying, but before I did, I told Boss one last important thing, what I'd almost forgot, the last thing I ever said to him while he was alive. I wanted to tell him how to find her. I thought of her blonde cropped hair, the eyes the color of Luca's, the peace I knew would have settled into her face. None of it felt unique enough though, until I remembered. "You'll know it's her," I told him, "because she'll smell just like me."

A Letter from Me to You

A reader sent me a message recently. Her friend had been through a loss. "How have you done it," she asked me, "because I'd like to tell her. How have you stayed so positive?" The first thing I did was check to make sure she had meant to send this message to me. The second thing I did was doubt everything I've ever written. Was it possible I had messed this up so bad, screwed up so royally that I'd given the impression that one, it is possible to have always stayed positive in the face of great loss and two, I'd somehow done it?

So if you have made it this far, dear reader, I hope you know this, but just in case, I will say it anyway: I have not done it. I have not stayed positive. I have been knocked down and knocked around and knocked out by life and loss, and I've spent great stretches of my life lying bleeding on the bathroom floor with no ability to even fathom how I would be able to get up, much less how I would ever be okay again. And yet—and if there is anything I am proud of in my life, anything I hope you can take away from this book at all, it is this—I did get up. Eventually.

But know too that I didn't write these stories from the bathroom floor. I wrote these stories once the bleeding had stopped and the wounds had closed and I was able to stand again without the pain knocking me over. I wrote these stories when I looked at myself and my life in the mirror after the losses, and realized that my pieces hadn't come together quite right, not like they were before. I was like a whole bunch of broken bones that hadn't set neatly back together. This is what loss will do to you: it will shatter who you think you are into pieces, and then your job, your only job in that moment, is to try to put yourself back together in a way that makes sense. For some of us, that may look like writing; for others, it may look like something else entirely. For none of us will it ever be easy or entirely pleasant, but I found when I'd pulled all the pieces back into a configuration that looked like a Liz that could maybe carry me forward, was that I was better for it.

Also, and this is important: it's not over. This life is a series of loves and losses filled in with long stretches of daily minutiae and sprinkled with moments of astounding joy. As I write this, it is September, and I can feel it again: the pull of the seasons changing, the shortening of the days, the darkening of the light. This month I will celebrate my birthday, like usual, and then two days later I will honor the anniversary of my mother's death, and throughout I will try not to get swept up in and under the tidal wave of depression that can come this time of year for me.

So no, having lived through these loves and losses has not given me any armor against the darkness. In all honesty, it's probably left me more vulnerable to it, at least temporarily, in the way that a piece of pottery that has been glued back together will always be fragile along its new seams. I know there will be times in my life where I will break again, as we all will. But what I have now is more valuable than any armor: I have the faith that I will be able to come back together again when I need to. The only thing more powerful than the darkness is the light, and the only thing more powerful than the light is the faith that the light is coming when you can't yet see it. And those seams that leave us delicate? They are the very places that the light shines first.

From the boundless depths of my broken and patched-up heart, thank you.

XOXO,

Liz

Acknowledgments

Years ago I sat down to write a story about my mother, and it became a story about motherhood. To that end I'd like to thank the village that helped mother this story as it grew up. To Emily Brower and the whole team at Broadleaf books, thank you for taking my words and shaping them into a book. To Angela Scheff and the Christopher Ferebee Agency, thank you for taking a risk on me and my little story and helping me to believe in both. To Shelby Spear for making me that first essential connection and to all of the amazing writers who I'm lucky enough to call friends even if we have never met in real life, thank you for letting me vent and then reminding me to shut up and write. To the women in my life who have mothered me when my own mother couldn't: my sister Katherine, my dear Aunt, my saint of a mother in law Dolores, Kate, Kelly, Stef, Megan, Jocelyn, Jessica, and so many others: there but for the support of you, go I. And of course to my dad, who faithfully read my words even when they made him uncomfortable. To Nick, Jack, Maria, Gabrielle, and Luca: thank you for everything, full stop. You're the reason I found the strength to get back up, every single time. And to Linda, my beautiful mother: every word I've ever written has been for you, and it will never be enough to truly thank you.